PRENTICE HALL SERIES IN WORLD RELIGIONS

ROBERT S. ELLWOOD, EDITOR

William R. LaFleur

University of California
Los Angeles

BUDDHISM: a cultural perspective

PRENTICE HALL, Englewood Cliffs, New Jersey 07632

Library of Congress Cataloging-in-Publication Data

LaFleur, William R.
    Buddhism: a cultural perspective.

    Bibliography: p. 146
    Includes index.
    1. Buddhism. I. Title.
BQ4012.L33 1988   294.3   87-2320
ISBN 0-13-084724-0

Editorial/production supervision: Marianne Peters
Interior and cover design: Maureen Eide
Manufacturing buyer: Peter Havens

For Jeannemarie,
Michael, and David

© 1988 by Prentice-Hall, Inc.
A Division of Simon & Schuster
Englewood Cliffs, New Jersey 07632

Printed in the United States of America

10 9 8 7 6 5 4

ISBN 0-13-084724-0

Prentice-Hall International (UK) Limited, *London*

Prentice-Hall of Australia Pty. Limited, *Sydney*

Prentice-Hall Canada Inc., *Toronto*

Prentice-Hall Hispanoamericana, S.A., *Mexico*

Prentice-Hall of India Private Limited, *New Delhi*

Prentice-Hall of Japan, Inc., *Tokyo*

Simon & Schuster Asia Pte. Ltd., *Singapore*

Editora Prentice-Hall do Brasil, Ltda., *Rio de Janeiro*

Contents

part 1

BUDDHISM AND CULTURE IN HISTORY

part 2

ANALYSIS OF THE BUDDHIST TRADITION: THE THREE TREASURES

Foreword

The Prentice Hall Series in World Religions is a new set of introductions to the major religious traditions of the world, which intends to be distinctive in two ways: (1) Each book follows the same outline, allowing a high level of consistency in content and approach. (2) Each book is oriented toward viewing religious traditions as "religious cultures" in which history, ideologies, practices, and sociologies all contribute toward constructing "deep structures" that govern peoples' world view and life-style. In order to achieve this level of communication about religion, these books are not chiefly devoted to dry recitations of chronological history or systematic exposition of ideology, though they present overviews of these topics. Instead the books give considerable space to "cameo" insights into particular personalities, movements, and historical moments that encourage an understanding of the world view, life-style, and deep dynamics of religious cultures in practice as they affect real people.

Religion is an important element within nearly all cultures and itself has all the hallmarks of a full cultural system. "Religious culture" as an integrated complex includes features ranging from ideas and organization to dress and diet. Each of these details offers some insight into the meaning of the whole as a total experience and construction of a total "reality." To look at the religious life of a particular country or tradition in this way, then, is to give proportionate attention to all aspects of its manifestation: to thought, worship, and social organization; to philosophy and folk beliefs; to liturgy and pilgrimage; to family life, dress, diet, and the role of religious specialists like monks and shamans. This series hopes to instill in the minds of readers the ability to view religion in this way.

I hope you enjoy the journeys offered by these books to the great heartlands of the human spirit.

Robert S. Ellwood, editor
University of Southern California

Preface

I vividly recall a conversation that I had several years ago with a fellow American who claimed to be very attracted to Buddhism. He qualified this by saying that it was not so much Buddhism which appealed to him but rather the ideas of the Buddha. The problem with these ideas, he said, is that later on in history they lost their original purity when the teachings of the Buddha became involved with Indian thought and culture. He felt that especially when the ideas of the Buddha became entangled with a specific culture the message of the Buddha had already been lost, submerged in things with which it really should have had nothing to do.

I always felt there was something peculiar in that argument, although at the time I was at a loss to say what it was. This book, at least in some sense, is my response to that person. His point of view is interesting and not at all uncommon. Since hearing it from him I have heard it from many others. Nevertheless, I think this shows a misunderstanding of Buddhism, and so I begin this book by expressing my strong doubt that such a thing as Buddhism apart from the cultures of man has ever existed. This is not to say that there is not universal appeal and applicability in Buddhism's teachings. It simply means that such universality has always been communicated through the specific languages of specific peoples. Culture and articulation within culture were part of Buddhism from the very beginning—not something that was added or picked up later. Śākyamuni, the man often referred to as the founder of Buddhism, was an Indian who thought and acted like an Indian. To ignore that fact or to assume that the message of the Buddha only became involved with Indian thought and culture at some later point in its history will tend to give a peculiar shape to one's understanding of this religious philosophy. It will also obscure much of the richness in it.

This book, then, will unabashedly take a cultural perspective. It will do that in spite of the fact that many existing books on Buddhism seem, either explicitly or by their silence on the matter, to describe a Buddhism virtually disassociated from the cultures in which it historically existed. Though from the beginning Buddhism has been implicated with cultures and with specific thought-patterns, during its long history it made impressive jumps from one culture to another. To say that it is cultural does not mean that it cannot move from one culture to another; this book assumes the possibility of communication across cultures. Thus we begin with Buddhism's involvement in the culture and thought of India. We will then try to observe it as it moves elsewhere into very different contexts: China, Southeast Asia, Tibet, Japan, and even the West in more recent years. Culture is not ancillary to true Buddhism. It is neither the quirk of the anthropologist nor merely the every-day context into which an otherwise lofty and pure teaching got forced by time and circumstance. Culture, in short, is part of Buddhism's essence since it is part of man's.

Having said that, a few other things need to be noted. One is that this book will try—as much as is possible in the case of something so vast as a "world" religion—to accept the diversity within Buddhism. In order to do this, it is necessary to give roughly equal treatment to the two major traditions within Buddhism, now usually referred to as the Theravada and the Mahayana. Obviously all the schools and sub-schools cannot receive equal time and attention. If there are readers already familiar with some things in Buddhism, they are sure to feel that their favorite thinker or school has been overlooked or given too little mention here. I have tried to give balanced attention to the various cultures in which Buddhism has found itself. In addition I hope the occasional shift of focus from the Theravada to the Mahayana and back again will not be too confusing. The intention is to express the differences as well as the continuities within the two traditions. As regards the Mahayana tradition I have sometimes let Ch'an or Zen stand out against the background of the whole of the Mahayana. The reason for this is that, although Zen has even become an English word, the general understanding of it in the West still remains unsatisfactory.

The study of Buddhism necessarily means learning some new, initially unfamiliar, words. Specialists in this area of study usually dress these words, no matter from what language they are taken, with important diacritical marks—things that look like dots, dashes, slashes, and apostrophes on words in our otherwise familiar Roman type. Although an attempt has been made to keep the introduction of new words within reasonable limits, I have kept the diacriticals on some words. Other words, however, have already made their way into our dictionaries; there they usually appear shorn of the marks specialists like to see on them. I see no need, however, to make foreign again what the dictionary—in this case *Webster's New Collegiate Dictionary*—has already given us as a new word in our *own* language. Thus this book will write Pali rather than Pāli and nirvana rather than nirvāṇa. In the course of this book new foreign words will appear in italics only the first time. Specialists know that the Indian vocabulary of Buddhism comes from two languages, Sanskrit and Pali. Here words in the text will usually appear in Sanskrit. Some Pali words of fairly common usage and on the verge of acceptance into our dictionary have been used in the text itself.

One more point deserves a note here. Although I have focussed on Buddhism in culture, I have attempted also to envision the particular problems faced by a Western student who is trying to grasp its often elusive concepts and formulations. Although the world continues to "shrink" and contact between diverse peoples becomes ever easier, I think it remains that, for a great variety of reasons, Buddhism is still a difficult and opaque form of religious philosophy for Westerners. Even the need to refer to it as a "religious philosophy" suggests the problem since we usually do not know exactly how to classify it. Is it a religion, or is it a philosophy? In colleges and universities you might find it taught in either kind of department. This ambiguity is positive in part because the study of Buddhism makes us think anew about these two categories of human experience, and how they interconnect in cultural traditions quite different from those of the West. One thing the study of Buddhism can do is to force us to ask at what point a philosophy becomes a religion and where a religion becomes a philosophy.

Here I will merely leave the problem in place, not try to solve it. An observation by Alfred North Whitehead in 1926, however, has always seemed appropriate to me. In his essay "Religion in the Making" he wrote that "Christianity . . . has always been a religion seeking a metaphysic [or philosophy], in contrast to Buddhism which is a metaphysic generating a religion." The point I especially like about Whitehead's formula is that it makes a provocative contrast but keeps it relative rather than absolute. He also allows for a creative tension in both contexts. His statement can also be used in looking at specific developments in the history of Buddhism within cultures. I recommend that upon completion of this book the reader return again to Whitehead's statement and give it further consideration.

The writing of this book took longer than I ever anticipated, but it also proved much more enjoyable than I had ever thought. I thank Robert S. Ellwood for giving me the idea, the framework, and the challenge. I thank my teachers at the University of Chicago some fifteen years ago—Professors Joseph M. Kitagawa, Charles H. Long, Frank E. Reynolds, Anthony C. Yu, Jonathan Z. Smith and especially the late Professor Mircea Eliade—for a now incalculable contribution to the things I now value. Masao Abe, whom I first met at Chicago, contributed greatly both then and subsequently to my study of Buddhism.

William R. LaFleur

overview: bangkok and its buddhas

It was my first visit to Thailand and I knew that I could spend only a week there. Half a student and half a pilgrim, I wanted to see as much of Thai Buddhism as I could during that short time. Having scarcely landed in Bangkok, I found a taxi and a driver who had the bare necessities of English and told him some of the famous, great temples of the city I especially wished to see—places such as Wat Po and Wat Sutat. From photos I had seen earlier, I knew I would be impressed by the extraordinary calm and tranquility of the golden Buddha images I would find inside the various temples. What I had not at all expected, however, was what my taxi driver did. After he had found a parking place close to each temple we visited, I expected him to stay in his taxi, taking advantage of a few minutes to catch up on sleep while I was inside. But to my surprise he followed me inside each temple we visited. It was not that he wanted to be my guide; his English was not good enough to enable that. It seemed that he wanted to accompany me. He was simply another pilgrim just a couple of steps behind me. Even when I laid out a few coins to buy thin filaments of gold leaf to attach to the gilded Buddha images, he too took from his cabbie's fare something so as to make his own offering at each temple. Standing before each seated or reclining image, I put my palms together in front of my chest in the gesture called *añjali* in much of the Buddhist world. (In Japan, where I had most of my contact with Buddhism, this was called the *gasshō* bow.) Each time I did this the taxi driver did the same. At first it was a bit disconcerting. Then I recalled something told me some months earlier by a Buddhist monk in Japan, namely, that even though certain images are commonly referred to as "Buddhas," such compositions of wood, stone, or gold are really no more "enlightened" (the root meaning of *bodh* from which our word "Buddha" comes) than any man, woman, or child in the universe. He had told me that the Buddha whom we respect with a bow is really the enlightenment that is in all of us and in everything. Recalling this while making the rounds of Bangkok temples, I felt that the taxi driver following me and joining me in bowing in front of the icons was himself a Buddha. Thus, during my tour of temples that afternoon, I had a Buddha in front of me on the altar and also a Buddha behind me in work clothes and rubber sandals. What at first had distracted me turned out to be something that added greatly to my sense of reverence and respect as I visited the Bangkok temples that hot afternoon.

That evening I had dinner with an old friend, a Japanese professor who had been living in Bangkok for some years. He had been teaching the Japanese language and courses in Japanese cultural history to Thai students at Chulalongkorn University in the Thai capital. I mentioned to him my experience of the afternoon, how surprised and then pleased I had been with the taxi driver who had joined me in paying homage at the temples of that city. My friend said that this fit his own experience exactly and that it showed how deeply pious the Thai people are in their devotion to Buddhism. He went on to say that, although as a Japanese he had always thought of himself as a Buddhist in some sense, his residence in Bangkok had repeatedly reminded him that, because their cultures are so different, so too the Buddhism of Japan and the Buddhism of Thailand differ considerably. An expression of devotion to what are called the Three Treasures—the *Buddha* as enlightened one, the *dharma* as the revered teaching, and the *sangha* as the community that follows these teachings—can be found throughout the Buddhist world, but even these basic terms can be understood and interpreted quite differently in different cultural contexts.

To illustrate his point, he told me of an experience he himself had had one day while teaching his students in Bangkok. He had been giving them a lecture on

Head of Buddha, Thailand

the Buddhist art of eighth-century Japan and, in order to help explain the sculpture of that period, had brought along a large photograph of one especially fine Buddhist image in the Japanese city of Nara. He had set up this photo in front of the class and, with pointer in hand, was discussing some of the details of artistic execution in the work. After he had been doing this for some minutes, one of the students in the class bolted upright at his own desk and, looking very distressed, said, "Excuse me for interrupting, Professor! But we are getting nervous when you take that pointer and use it to touch the arms and eyes of the Buddha. Teacher, please do not point at the Buddha! We Thais only want to bow to the Buddha. We don't want to touch his face with that piece of wood." With that, he made the añjali bow and his classmates rose as a group to do the same from their respective seats. Recovering from his initial surprise, my friend, their Japanese professor, realized exactly what had happened and responded by himself making a bow to the photo of the icon. As a Japanese, he regards himself as a Buddhist, but he is also deeply sensitive to the cultural differences among Buddhists; in this case, he realized that his students were teaching him something important about these variations within the Buddhist world.

The difference here is very interesting. It might be explained in part—but only in part—by a difference between the sensitivities of a very modernized people and a people with more traditional attitudes and ways of thinking. The late Paul Mus, a French scholar and perceptive observer of Asian cultures, noted some years ago that there is a tremendous difference between a religious painting or image in a temple and that same icon when it has been transported to a museum. He wrote that when we take Buddhist, Hindu, or even medieval Christian images out of their original settings and mount them for display in our modern galleries or museums, our attitude about them is remarkably different from the attitude of the people who revered them originally in temples or on private altars in their own homes. Mus noted that most of us in today's West are modern and take for granted a distinction between religious things and aesthetic things. When we take an image from its original setting, we isolate it for what we want to be a merely artistic appreciation.[1] Then we begin to think of them as "works of art," begin to notice details of their composition and execution, and compare their finesse and beauty with other pieces of art. We put them in glass cases, flood them with artificial light, photograph them for exhibition catalogues, and feel little or no hesitation in using our fingers as pointers to call attention to details we think worthy of comment. This is all part of what we call the "appreciation" of art. But it is, of course, far removed from the way such images or pictures were originally respected and revered by the devotee who bowed reverently before them in local temples and shrines.

In part, this explains why my Japanese friend so inadvertently shocked his Thai students. Although in Japan, too, there are many temples and even places in private homes where a Buddha image is properly addressed with a reverential bow,

---

[1] Paul Mus, "Thousand-Armed Kannon—A Mystery or a Problem?" *Journal of Indian and Buddhist Studies*, Vol. 12, no. 1 (1964), 470–438 (reverse pagination is correct).

Japan today also has many galleries and salesrooms of art. In such contexts it is common for works of Buddhist sculpture to be exhibited, discussed, pointed at, and—in the showrooms—even marketed. So my friend's lecture to his university students had been based on that assumption; he simply did not expect that his descriptions of technique and his use of a wooden pointer in class would be regarded by his students as an act of impiety or sacrilege. Certainly the gap between acts of reverence in traditional cultures and acts of art appreciation in more modern ones explains part of the difference between my friend and his students—even though both he and they would regard themselves as Buddhists.

But there is much more. This was not the first or the last time that Buddhists from one part of Asia bewildered or even shocked those from another part with "outlandish" ideas or behavior. Buddhism, after all, has been part of Asian life for at least twenty-five hundred years, having taken shape largely from the life and teachings of an Indian prince named Śākyamuni who lived approximately from 560 to 480 B.C.E. From such beginnings in India and over the next two and a half millennia, Buddhism penetrated into every Asian land to the east of what we now call Afghanistan and, at least since the nineteenth century, also has become part of the thinking and practice of some people in Europe and America as well. When we think of it as having made a slight move into the West in recent years, we recognize that this involves a jump across an immense cultural gap, but in some sense, it may be no greater than what happened two thousand years ago when Buddhism moved across the physical and cultural differences between India and China. Sometimes we in the West loosely talk about "the mind of Asia" or "Eastern spirituality" as if there were a great commonality in the largest land mass of the world. But in fact the various cultures of Asia are vastly different from one another and the cultural gap between India and China is as great as any in the world. There was also such a gap in the first century of the common era when Buddhism, till then something indelibly stamped as Indian, began the process of entering into Chinese society, thought forms, literary traditions, and cultural patterns. This was to turn out to be something that probably ranks as one of the most significant and interesting instances of cultural exchange in human history.

And it is something that is in some way connected with the difference between the Thai and the Japanese attitudes with respect to the image of the Buddha. The Buddhism of Thailand, like that of Sri Lanka, Burma, Cambodia, and Laos, is primarily of the Theravada (Way of the Elders) school, whereas that of Japan, like that of Korea, Mongolia, China, Tibet, and Vietnam, is primarily of that which is called the Mahayana (Greater Vehicle). Naturally, within both the Theravada and the Mahayana there are many subdivisions and divergences, usually referred to as "schools" rather than "sects." There are differences in doctrine, but much of the time it is in the area of practice—or how Buddhists go about being Buddhists in everyday life—that these come to the surface. Because Asia is so vast and because travel from one part to another is often so difficult, the passage of many centuries gave the various peoples there ample opportunity to develop their own distinctive forms of Buddhism—often in response to differences in climate, ecology, language,

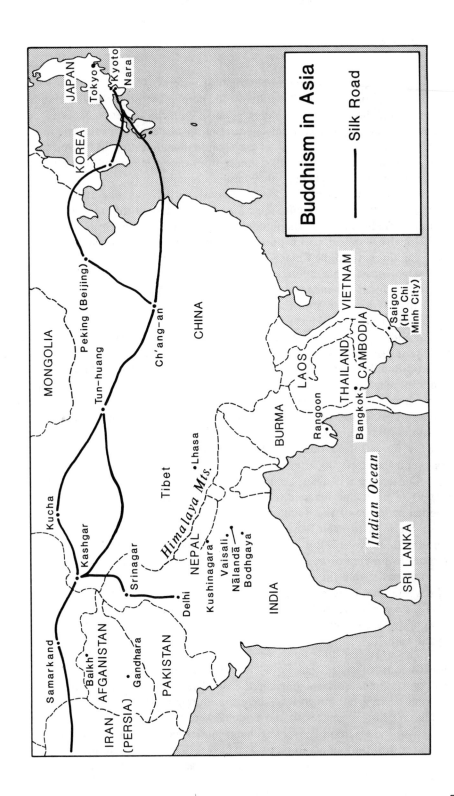

Buddhism in Asia

—— Silk Road

JAPAN
Tokyo • Kyoto • Nara

KOREA

Peking (Beijing) •

Ch'ang-an •

Tun-huang •

MONGOLIA

CHINA

Kucha •

Kashgar •

Srinagar •

Delhi •

Samarkand •

Balkh •

AFGANISTAN

Gandhara •

IRAN
(PERSIA)

PAKISTAN

Himalaya Mts.

Tibet

• Lhasa

NEPAL

Kushinagara •
Vaisali •
Nālandā •
Bodhgaya •

INDIA

BURMA

Rangoon •

LAOS

THAILAND

Bangkok •

VIETNAM

CAMBODIA

Saigon
(Ho Chi
Minh City) •

Indian Ocean

SRI LANKA

preexisting religious forms, and philosophical systems. There is, moreover, no central organizing unit for the Buddhist world—no papacy, no ecclesiastical judiciary, no procedure nowadays for holding periodic councils to settle issues of debate, and no holy city quite like Rome, Jerusalem, or Mecca. Within the twentieth century, of course, the greater ease of travel and communication has meant that even Theravada and Mahayana Buddhists meet from time to time and try to understand how they differ and what things they have in common.

But some paragraphs back we left only partially answered the problem of why the Thais and the Japanese *as Buddhists* had such different attitudes with respect to Buddha images. The Buddhism of the Japanese was that called Mahayana or the one that spread across a northern course in Asia. The Japanese learned how to be Buddhists from the Chinese and the Koreans, and their Buddhism had already undergone considerable cultural adaptation in East Asia. My Japanese friend, therefore, was himself the inheritor of an attitude about Buddhist images that was not at all that of his Thai students. For in one of the most important schools of the Mahayana or Greater Vehicle, the school known as Ch'an to the Chinese and as Zen in both Japan and the West, there was both the customary great reverence for Buddha images and also the development of something that can only be called a kind of Buddhist iconoclasm. Actually, this was part of a Buddhist critique of Buddhist religiosity. (It should not be mistaken for the all-too-easy "hip Zen" with which some Westerners have confused it, because it arises only *after* there has been a good deal of reverence for expressions of Buddha-hood in metal, wood, and stone.) But many of these Chinese Buddhists were very wary about the mind's capacity for self-deception; they were happy to bow and then quickly remember that wood and stone are, after all, wood and stone—no more, no less!

Concerning T'ien-jan, a ninth-century Chinese monk, for instance, it is said that while practicing his meditations during one especially cold night, he took a wooden sculpture of the Buddha from the temple altar, chopped it up, and kindled it for firewood to keep himself warm. This shocked his fellow monks, and they censured him severely. But T'ien-jan responded with the claim that he had done so in order to procure *śarīra*, a residue in the ashes that was traditionally thought to be a holy relic from the cremated body of a Buddha. "But how," his interlocutors asked, "did you expect to get the relic of the Buddha by burning something that is only a piece of wood?" To this T'ien-jan replied: "Aha! But if it is only a piece of wood, why are you so upset with me for burning it when I needed heat to keep myself warm?!"

The story has both humor and an important point. The latter is especially clear when it is recalled that throughout the centuries, Buddhists have had an especially great fondness for expressing their understanding of Buddha-hood in sculpture and painting. Although it is likely that during the first couple of centuries of Buddhism's history images of the Buddha were not made, the evidence from all the rest of the tradition is overwhelming: images were multiplied, and the making of images was itself an act of piety. The images themselves communicated the Buddhist ideal of a human life made tranquil and peaceful through meditation, analysis, discernment, and the practice of a life of selflessness. It is very clear that throughout history—and even today—people in the presence of such an image have experienced a readiness to let its tranquility communicate something of the same to their own minds.

The burning of images and a bold readiness to trample on holy things for the sake of something regarded as even more precious and worthy of respect is, even in Zen, something that may be done only by those who are truly enlightened. In Japan, Ikkyū (1394–1481) was considered to be such. His accomplishments as a poet, painter, and man of Zen were monumental. But Ikkyū was also a bold Buddhist iconoclast. One tale told about him typifies the popular understanding of Ikkyū as man of Zen. One day when a new Buddhist image had just been completed for a new temple in a local village, Ikkyū was invited to perform what is called the "eye-opening" ceremony; as a famous Zen monk, it was appropriate for him to paint in the final touch, the "eyes" that would make the image seem lifelike. But upon his arrival there, Ikkyū climbed up on the immaculately clean altar and, while the faithful watched to see how he would perform the ceremony, lifted the front hem of his monk's robe and proceeded to urinate on the new icon. The shock among the faithful was, of course, great, and it took some time for the people to realize why the enlightened monk had acted with what seemed to be such outrageous impiety.[2] In fact, Ikkyū was merely giving a dramatic and bold expression to something often said by Buddhists, namely, that "the Buddha" will be lost if it is projected on to something or someone *out there!* For many Buddhists, this is what has happened when an image has become an idol; it has begun to prevent rather than facilitate the realization of a person's own Buddha-hood.

Buddhism has often been called "the gentle faith." This perhaps refers to the fact that it has usually seemed somehow unseemly to Buddhists to take up arms to fight for their religion; the notion of any kind of holy war has historically been repugnant to Buddhists. In addition, they have generally—although certainly not always—been reluctant to vilify one another even when genuine differences of concept and practice came into being. There have been cases of strong sectarianism, but on the other hand, many Buddhist teachers have encouraged their students to go out and learn firsthand from a variety of teachers, not just from themselves. The impulse to disparage the religious beliefs and practices of non-Buddhists has been usually kept under a fair amount of control as well; even as it radiated out from India to other cultures of Asia, Buddhism usually entered quite quickly into some kind of peaceful symbiosis with other forms of philosophy and religion in those new lands. It usually did not try to expunge or erase them.

But this is not to say that points of tension cannot be detected in its history or that the entry and presence of Buddhism in lands other than India was always an easy one. Much of this book will investigate these issues—in part because we can often learn much about the nature of a particular religion or philosophy by looking at how it interacts with others and tries to solve problems that exist within itself.

---

[2] James H. Sanford, *Zen-Man Ikkyū* (Chico, Calif.: Scholars Press, 1981), pp. 291–295.

The emphasis here, as noted, will be upon the expression of Buddhism in specific cultural forms. This connection with culture exists, moreover, from the first days of a specific religion. In the case of Buddhism, it seems to us important to note that even its founder, Śākyamuni, was an Indian who shared many—although not necessarily all—the assumptions of Indian culture. Certainly Śākyamuni had a message that he and his followers have held to be applicable to all mankind. Nevertheless, it is one that arose within the context of *Indian* religious thought and, even when undergoing vast changes in other cultures, seems to have carried down with it through the centuries some imprint from Indian life and thinking.

This does not mean that a given culture is uniform, always and everywhere the same. When dealing with something so large as Buddhism, a "world" religion that has passed into very diverse cultures in its long history, it is natural for the student of the subject to want to get a mental handle on each of the cultures involved. It is tempting then to try to characterize each culture in terms of a few things taken as dominant traits—to somehow fix the "national character" of each culture and then expect to watch how the newcomer from the outside—Buddhism in this case—passed into that culture and itself took on what we have taken to be that culture's dominant traits. In this model the cultures are like sieves and the incoming element, even when it is a powerful religious and philosophical system, is seen as passing through and having its "foreign" elements gradually removed and discarded—just the way a filter or sieve deals with physical objects that are too large to pass through it. The problem with this culture-as-sieve model is that it takes the recipient cultures as frozen or fixed in time, themselves unalterable. Only the new, incoming ideas and cultural elements are taken as changeable, and they, to the extent that they continue to exist in their new setting, are taken as a thin "veneer" on that old culture and unable to enter deeply into it. In this book, however, we will assume that *both* parties in such interactions can change with time and sufficient reason to do so. We assume that at certain times in history, the people of one culture may be very fascinated with another—so much so that they imbibe large doses of the other and undergo cultural change themselves as a result. Our model of the connection between cultures and change should allow for many and various possibilities.

The notion of "national character" can also lead to misunderstandings, especially when it is summarized in simple formulas. For instance, it is possible to read books, especially older books or even contemporary books that have the traveler in view, that oversimplify things as follows: the Indians are depicted as philosophical but are also introverted and sad; by contrast, the Chinese are described as pragmatic, extroverted, and sanguine in their disposition. Then in such books when Buddhism is mentioned, it is said to have been transformed from a pessimistic and philosophical faith to an optimistic and practical one when it was passed from the Indians to the Chinese. Or else the Indians are taken as "world-negating" and the Chinese and Japanese as "world-affirming"; then Buddhism's passage from South Asia to East Asia is described simply as the switch from negation to affirmation of the world. The basic problem in this is the one of oversimplification, of taking things fairly complicated—and certainly both history and culture are complex—and reducing these things to a few mental handles. It overlooks the wide variety of personality types that may be found within a single culture. Then, for example, it neglects to look at the fact that Indians are fully capable of thinking and acting in practical ways and that the Chinese are equally capable of doing complex, even introspective philosophy.

Therefore, although here we will be interested in Buddhism in the context of specific cultures and their characteristic problems, we will try to avoid simplistic formulas and judgments that are easy and tempting—but often wrong. In looking at the twenty-five hundred years of Buddhist history, we will assume that Buddhism made a considerable impact upon the cultures it touched and also at the same time that Buddhism too was greatly impacted by the peoples and cultures it took up with during its long history.

2

a history
of buddhism

ALWAYS THERE: THE OPEN ENDS OF HISTORY

This chapter will be largely historical; it will take up the basics of the life of the man usually referred to when the term "Buddha" is used to point to one specific individual living within a specific time in world history. But before giving the account of his life, something needs to be said about the way in which most Buddhists themselves view this aspect of their own history. Specifically, we need to note that Buddhists do not claim to be possessors of any "revelation" in the sense of some news or information divulged or delivered to humankind from some extra-human or supernatural source. Gods, as we shall see, do not have an important role to play in Buddhism, and as a result, there is no real role for divine revelations to man either. What the Buddhists do regard as crucially important, however, is what they call the *dharma*. The content of this will be discussed in Chapter 5, and it is true that the word "dharma" has many meanings and uses. But most often it refers to what at bottom is true, real, and reliable about man and the universe. It is what you have left over after conducting the most thoroughgoing analysis—sometimes while doing meditation—to clear away and dispense with all the falsehoods, fabrications, and half-truths that people hold in their minds and use for shaping—or just as likely misshaping—their lives. The Buddhists share in one of the general suppositions of Indian culture in holding that the dharma is *always there* underneath all the delusions we manufacture; it is like the moon hidden behind a bank of clouds or like the mountain that is temporarily obscured by mist and fog. (It is no accident that these are a couple of the most favored metaphors in Buddhism.) When the veils of falsehood are removed through "enlightenment" or an "awakening," it is the dharma that can be seen in all its clarity and solidity. The important thing, at least to the Buddhists, is that it always was there, is there, and will be there. It does not come into being at a certain point in history and does not ever pass away—even though our own human awareness of it may be dimmed during certain periods of our history. Time neither makes nor breaks the dharma; history too does not seriously affect it.

This "always there" characteristic of the dharma is, according to the Buddhists, part and parcel of its universality. And this universality is taken very literally and portrayed very pictorially: the dharma is the Truth that always was and always will be at the inner structure of the universe or cosmos, in all places and in all time frames. Being Indians, the early Buddhists immediately thought of the universe in terms of vast immensity and as a frame within which many world-systems exist. The distance of other worlds and times from our own was customarily measured in terms of the *kalpa*,[1] a unit of time equal to 4,320,000,000 of our years.

Therefore, when the early Buddhists of India talked about a man whom they had personally known and who had been for them an unparalleled teacher, they called him the enlightened one or "the Buddha." He is someone who we today estimate must have lived roughly between 560 and 480 B.C.E. But the important thing to notice is that the Indian Buddhists did not regard him as the one and only Buddha; rather, they regarded him as one among many Buddhas or enlightened ones. He was the one closest to them—and even the closest to us today—in time and space, but, precisely because according to them the dharma is universal and pervading the universe, the early Buddhists simply assumed that the dharma could not possibly have begun with him. According to their logic, it had to be older, much older—as old as the universe itself. It extended far beyond the reaches of our most ambitious imagination, and, since it was the habit of the Buddhists to refrain from thinking of the universe as having a definite point of beginning, this meant that the dharma was very old indeed!

The implications of this were profound. For one thing, this meant that their Buddha, the one they themselves knew and talked with, had not just happened into history but had been prepared for this life during earlier lives. He had, they assumed, undergone intense preparatory training for his present life by being taught by other Buddhas in other worlds and other time frames. To these early Buddhists, this was not a matter of speculation or conjecture; as Indians, the matter of living multiple lives—what we sometimes call "rebirth," "metempsychosis," or "reincarnation"—was simply *assumed* to be true. It was part of the basics of their minds and culture, an implicit assumption, not a "maybe" or a possibility. The fact of multiple lives seemed as certain to them as was the daily rising and setting of the sun.

So the question became: Where do we begin when we set out to tell the story of the "life" of the Buddha? If we begin with a date somewhere around 560 B.C.E.,

---

[1] David R. Kinsley, *Hinduism: A Cultural Perspective* (Englewood Cliffs, N.J.: Prentice-Hall, 1982), p. 86.

we will already have twisted what most Buddhists believe out of shape to some extent and refashioned it to fit the contour, presuppositions, and expectations of *our* culture. If we begin the historical account in the sixth century B.C.E., we will already have shaved off an immensely important prehistory, the kalpas of time when the dharma was already "there" and when other Buddhas—one named Dīpamkara, for instance—were the enlightened ones of their own aeons and were in their time and space frames busily involved in giving the necessary training to the one who would later be born in a place and time relatively close to us, that is, in India in the sixth century B.C.E. According to many Buddhists, that was when he became "our" Buddha, but he really existed much earlier as a *bodhisattva,* that is, a Buddha-to-be. It was as such that he was trained by Dīpamkara and other Buddhas in the cosmos. The important point is that, at least according to many Buddhists, those earlier lives were in an important sense also parts of his comprehensive biography; to chip them away because our culture does not share the same assumptions as the Indians is to chip away a piece of something very important to many Buddhists and to an understanding of this form of religious philosophy.

According to them, the only right way of talking about the "life" of the Buddha is to switch to the plural and talk about his "lives." Buddhists have usually done this through an entire genre of narratives, the *Stories of the Buddha's Previous Lives (Jātaka);*[2] some of these stories are as old as the second century B.C.E. and are believed to tell the story of how he made a slow but steady ascent up the ladder of being and rebirth until he was born and lived in India with the name of Śākyamuni (Sage of the Śākya clan). This slow ascent even involved earlier lives in nonhuman form. Many Buddhists believe that these stories are rooted in the preaching of the Buddha himself,[3] that is, lives that he, by virtue of the wonderful mental power that was part of his enlightenment, became able to remember and recollect. His mind had become one from which the fog of forgetfulness had been dissolved, and, it was assumed, he himself had told his companions the details of his earlier lives. After centuries of telling and retelling, these got to number 547 tales concerning 547 lifetimes and were collected most completely in Sri Lanka in the fifth century C.E. The modern skeptical mind will wonder about all of this and suspect that most or all of them are fabrications, stories of a later time that were appended to whatever original germ of truth was there. The traditional Buddhist, however—unless he or she too has been touched by the presuppositions of the modern West—usually holds these to be factual accounts.

---

[2] *Buddhist Birth Stories or Jātaka Tales,* trans. by T. W. Rhys Davids (Boston: Houghton Mifflin, 1880).

[3] Frank E. Reynolds, "The Many Lives of the Buddha: A Study of Sacred Biography and Theravāda Tradition," in Frank E. Reynolds and Donald Capps, eds., *The Biographical Process: Studies in the History and Psychology of Religion* (The Hague and Paris: Mouton, 1976), pp. 37–61. See also Richard Gombrich, "The Significance of Former Buddhas in the Theravādin Tradition," in Somaratna Balasooriya, ed., *Buddhist Studies in Honor of Walpola Rahula* (London: Gordon Fraser, and Sri Lanka: Vimamsa, 1980), pp. 62–72.

DEVELOPMENT: FROM ŚĀKYAMUNI TO THE BUDDHA

If it is understood that many Buddhists hold the wider view that there have been and will continue to be many Buddhas in the vastness of cosmic time and space, we may now narrow our focus and tell the basic events in the life of the Buddha who is both closest and most important to us—Śākyamuni.[4] At the end of the nineteenth century, many European scholars were very skeptical as to whether such a person had, in fact, ever lived. They thought that the whole of his life story might be a pious fiction, something concocted by a religious community, or maybe even a solar myth. Today, however, there is a general agreement that we need not be quite so skeptical. Although certainly the story of his life was elaborated and embellished by many retellings and the imagination of pious people, all the extant biographies seem to have been based on one lost one that was composed a little more than a century after his death. Scholars now also generally hold that the events narrated concerning the latter part of his life are far more trustworthy than are those about the earlier part.

But it is not necessary here to try to sort out the different levels of credibility. More important for us is to grasp the basic outline of the story of the Buddha that has captured the imagination of the Buddhist community for more than two thousand years and, for Buddhists, still serves as the paradigm of ideal human existence. Perhaps because Buddhism continues to bear the stamp of something that arose in India rather than in the history-conscious West, it is said by some contemporary Buddhists that the truth of this basic life *as paradigm* would remain true and compelling even if someone were to come along some day and prove definitively that Śākyamuni had never even lived. That is, according to Indian thinking, the truth of the universal paradigm is much more important than are any individual historical instances of it.

The life span of Śākyamuni began somewhere around the year 560 B.C.E. when he was born on the full-moon date of the fourth month as the son of Suddhodana and his wife Māyā. Suddhodana was the ruler of Kapilavastu, a city or town on the plain where the Ganges river meets the foothills of the Himalayan range. Pious tradition probably exalts his status considerably, telling us that he was a king and a person with immense wealth. Thus, his son's later renunciation of that status and wealth was made even more impressive. It also greatly exaggerates the nature of Śākyamuni's birth; the Jātaka tales say that his mother became pregnant when she had a dream of a white and wondrous elephant, that he was born from her side rather than through her birth canal, and that as a newborn infant, he immediately stood up, pointed skyward, and predicted to all that he would become a Buddha in this lifetime. One aged wise man is said to have confirmed this prophecy, but others predicted that he would become not a religious sage but a *cakravartin* or Wheel-Turning Monarch instead. This either-or prophecy becomes the fulcrum on

---

[4] Another frequently used name is Gautama (Gotama).

which the future hinges. The narratives make clear that his father, Suddhodana, preferred the royal career for his son and was determined to do evertything in his power to prevent him from taking up a spiritual vocation. He circumscribed his son's life with guards and with pleasures, building three palaces for him, choosing a beautiful wife for him at age sixteen, and, according to the Jātakas, keeping him entertained with forty thousand dancing girls. But at age twenty-nine, the young man slipped outside the royal compound of his confinement and over four successive nights saw the "four signs," the very things from which his father wanted so desperately to shield him. This became the crucial turning point.

According to the account he was astonished to see four types of human conditions he had never before observed or known to exist: on the first night an old man bent with age, on the second a man riddled with disease, on the third a corpse, and on the fourth a serene-looking wandering monk. With each night's shocking new revelation of the real facts of human existence, the young Buddha-to-be's resolve to change the course of his own life became more fixed. It was precisely at this point in his life, however, that his wife gave birth to a son, something that ordinarily would have tied him much more to the householder's life. He immediately named the child "Impediment," thereby indicating that he had already resolved to break with life as husband, father, and householder. He retired to his harem that night, but in their sleep and nakedness, even his dancing girls seemed "like a cemetery filled with dead bodies," and he concluded that our multiple passions tend to turn our existence into "houses aflame with fire."

With this he decided that the pursuit of the highest dharma was most important, left the household once and for all, cut off his hair as a symbol of his new life, and began to walk the life path of a homeless monastic. At first he sought out some of the most famous spiritual and philosophical teachers of his time. He quickly and completely mastered the things they advocated, but still remained unsatisfied. Therefore, he turned to more severe and demanding practices. Having lived in the lap of luxury for twenty-nine years prior to his renunciation, he turned to the opposite extreme and became an ascetic yogi living in the forest. His practices there and his self-starvation took him to the point where his eyes were deeply sunken in his head and his body was just skin over bones. But he found that this did not satisfy his quest either and he received refreshing nectar from a young woman who took pity on him. This led him to discover something that he would later call the Middle Way. This discovery, the dharma, has among its characteristics the avoidance of the extreme of indulgence in pleasures and also the extreme of self-mortification. He discovered the truth that there is no abiding self or ego, that is, no trace of what the Indians in most of their philosophies called the *ātman*.

Then he went to the north of the forest to a place near the village of Bodh Gaya and sat down under a tree, vowing not to rise from that spot until he experienced complete enlightenment, the essence of *nirvana*. Sitting alone, he entered into the deepest of meditations. He was on the brink of the most important event in his long sequence of lives and in the history of Buddhism. On the night of his thirty-fifth birthday, another full-moon night, he was spiritually accosted by Māra, the powerful "Robber of Life" who is the personification of evil and is attended by a whole army of accomplices. That night the Buddha-to-be persevered through the most excruciating trials and temptations. But in the end he gained knowledge of all his previous existences, gained the "divine eye," and also fathomed the truth of what was to be called *pratītya-samutpāda* or dependent co-origination. His goal had finally been attained; he was now united with enlightenment, no longer a Buddha-to-be but a Buddha. Long kalpas of preparation had yielded their positive result; Śākyamuni himself knew the deepest dharma, the taste of nirvana.

The next question became one of what he now should do. For a number of weeks he stayed in deep meditation near the tree where the great event had taken place, a tree later to be called the Tree of Enlightenment and the parent of a tree that exists even today in Bodh Gaya. One tradition holds that a couple of merchants, laymen rather than monks, stopped to pay tribute to him and offer him rice and honey cakes. The gods immediately appeared and provided him with sapphire bowls to use for eating, but he refused these and chose humble bowls of stone instead. Sometime afterward, having hesitated to teach because he thought his own insight into the dharma too profound and difficult for ordinary folk to comprehend, he decided at last to give expression to what he had learned and mastered. Compassion for the suffering of other beings and his deep desire to lift them out of their misery compelled him to bring into being the sangha, that is, the community of those trying to follow the same path. At a place called Deer Park near the holy city of Benares, he addressed his first discourse to a group of mendicant monks.

This is known as the Sermon that Turns the Wheel (of the dharma). Its core is usually summarized in two formulas, the Four Noble Truths and the Eightfold Path. The former is Śākyamuni's insistence that spiritual liberation consists of coming to a realization of (1) the Truth of Suffering (*duḥkha*) and its pervasiveness in all beings, including ourselves; (2) the Truth of the Cause of Suffering as lying in our selfish cravings for pleasure, for perpetuation of our own existence, or for the illusion that we might somehow be exceptions to the law of impermanence; (3) the Truth of the Cessation of craving which is found by recognizing the vanity of our illusion of self and self-perpetuation and by living life consistent with this fact; and (4) the Truth of the Eightfold Path which leads to the eradication of suffering.

This fourth truth, logically, leads to the specification of the points of the Eightfold Path. It consists in (1) right seeing, (2) right thinking, (3) right speaking, (4) right action, (5) right livelihood, (6) right effort, (7) right mindfulness, and (8) right meditation. This also articulates the content of the Middle Path which stresses following the norms that Śākyamuni himself discovered to be "right" in the sense that they are those of the deepest dharma of the universe.

From this point on in the life of Śākyamuni, there were many places to visit and many sermons to preach. His life as an itinerant teacher lasted for the next forty-five years. Most Buddhists through history have believed that the sermons he preached on different occasions and to different audiences were remembered by disciples and later copied down. They became the *sutras* or scriptures of Buddhism. These record in specific detail the names of the people who became his disciples and the ongoing interaction between Śākyamuni and those disciples as he corrected their understanding of the dharma and encouraged them toward the liberation that he had come to know. Often these disciples appear in the sutras with distinctive and interesting traits of character: Ānanda, Śāriputra, Kāśyapa, and Maudgalyāyana are among the better known. Some of these were ascetics whom he had known earlier and who now, deeply impressed with the evidence of Śākyamuni's attainment, joined his sangha. Others were kings and influential citizens who sometimes joined the order as monks or nuns but more often as devout laypersons. These included even Śākyamuni's own father, Suddhodana, who earlier had so opposed his aspiration to seek enlightenment. Also Śākyamuni's son, the child born just as he was about to leave the householder's life, became a follower of his father, now the Buddha. According to the sutras, large numbers converted quickly to his teaching of the Middle Path. Lay patrons made it possible for the company of monks to live their modest livelihood without fear of starvation and added to the sangha's capacity for rapid growth.

When he was approximately eighty years old, Śākyamuni told his followers that he would soon die and was fully prepared to do so. The prospect of seeing him come to the end of his life was at first distressing to his disciples, but he chose to meet that end in a grove of trees near a small village named Kusinagara. He died there of an illness, but also expired in a manner typical of an Indian holy man— that is, through a series of meditative trances. His expiration is usually called the *parinirvāna,* that is, the nirvana that has been rounded out to complete perfection. Nothing especially miraculous happened at this point—other than the sudden bursting into white blossoms of the trees in the grove. Soon afterward his remains were cremated and the *śarīra* or residue, something that would be exceedingly precious to later generations, was placed in a stupa or mortuary mound with a small tower on top.

EXPANSION OF THE SANGHA

It was important that membership in the sangha be open to all. The Buddha did not recognize any special religious status or role in the brahmin or priestly caste of Indian society. This fact in itself meant that, although Buddhism was decidedly stamped by the Indian religious imagination and Indian culture from the very beginning, it at the same time fit somewhat oddly within the socioreligious composition of Indian culture, since caste there was taken to be something that is *religiously* significant. That is, the recognition of the brahmins as an elite class has also been the recognition of them as religious specialists who are born to that status. This has always[5] been intimately bound up with the nature of Hinduism itself.[5] For the Buddhists, however, this was not so. The brahmins as specialists in religious ritual were given no special recognition, and the opportunity to pursue the Path outlined by the Buddha was open to anyone of any caste whatsoever.

But, of course, this is also what made Buddhism very appealing to those who were not brahmins, and it is certainly no accident that the teachings of Śākyamuni were readily embraced by merchants, members of the military class, craftsmen, and other people in more "secular" vocations. By opening the pursuit of the Middle Path to any and everyone, the Buddha created a context wherein that path would be quite widely accepted. The number of persons ready to give up the householder's life and become a monk or nun, of course, was bound to be limited. But there was a much more vast population of people ready to be pious laypersons—supporters of the sangha, people who themselves were hoping to be born in another life where they themselves might become ascetics and aspire to be *arhats*—that is, persons who have realized enlightenment.

Likewise, in the early stage of Buddhism, there seems to have been a certain, though qualified, move in the direction of offering equality to women. The earliest texts tell the stories of women who attained perfect enlightenment through their own efforts and were qualified as arhats. The status of women in Buddhism will be considered further in Chapter 3; here, however, it is important to note that early in the history a fairly large number of women was attracted to Śākyamuni's teaching. The recognition of an intrinsic spiritual vocation in women, other than that which comes through child bearing or through serving as consorts and assistants to holy men, was also something that went against the grain of ancient Indian society—in fact, against the structure of all male-dominated societies in history. But it quite clearly seems to have been a dimension of the earliest sangha.

The monks were supposed to be in training to curb and then eliminate their cravings for physical things, for sex, for fame, or for experiences that gild and pamper the ego. Thus, their contact with women was carefully circumscribed; many of the sangha's rules deal with these matters. In addition, the monks were supposed to be itinerant and unburdened by a collection of worldly goods. Initially

---

[5] Kinsley, *Hinduism: A Cultural Perspective.*

their actual possessions, in fact, were supposed to be limited to the following items—a begging bowl, an extra robe, sandals, a razor for shaving the head, a needle, and a piece of gauze for straining liquids before drinking—so that the monk would not inadvertently take the life of small life forms that live unnoticed there. By this severe limitation of possessions they were expected to lead lives that were free of the burdens and cares of the ordinary householder; being "homeless" in this very radical and pervasive sense, they were meant to be free to give themselves fully to meditation, to the memorization and mastery of the vast canon of scriptures that was coming into existence, and to teaching junior monks or the laity who would gather to hear sermons.

Daily rice and other foodstuffs were received from householders or lay Buddhists on a begging round made by the monks each morning. Throughout much of the history of Buddhism—and in Sri Lanka and the nations of southeast Asia even today—this has been the hallmark of Buddhist culture. The monks made their rounds early in the day and provided the laity with an unparalleled opportunity to practice the virtue of *dāna,* that is, giving to the sangha, an act that at the same time is the first and major step in the layperson's move toward his or her own eventual nirvana. The monks would merely appear at the door of a home, receive a portion of food from what was prepared for the family that day, receive also the reverential and respectful bow of the layperson, and silently go on their way. When all the monks had returned to their temple or monastery, they would eat their meal in common—and do all the day's eating before noon so that the remainder of the day could be completely devoted to practice of the dharma. The begging bowl is an important Buddhist symbol; it encapsulates the ideals and freedom of the early sangha and serves also as a reminder of the long historical linkage between the monastic community and its lay supporters.

The most important layman in Buddhism—so important, in fact, that some say he should be ranked next to Śākyamuni in historical importance—was the emperor Asoka (ca. 274-232 B.C.E.). From his grandfather and father, Asoka had inherited a newly united India that stretched far in all directions. It remained for Asoka only to defeat one recalcitrant people, the Kaliṅgas. He did so, but the bloodbath this caused seems to have deeply bothered the emperor's conscience, and he felt the need to desist from any further warfare or conquests. Either because he found it to be an effective way of consolidating his gains or because he was sincerely interested in establishing a humanitarian rule (or perhaps a combination of both reasons), Asoka issued a large number of pronouncements. Because these were inscribed in stone and because many are extant and still legible today, the edicts of Asoka are often cited as one of the most impressive ethical statements of the ancient world. Asoka openly declared himself to be a lay follower of the Buddha, openly repented of the suffering he had caused by his earlier bellicosity, and declared that, unlike kings who go about their realms on "pleasure tours," he would travel through his own domain on "dharma tours" to promote justice, morality, and the welfare and harmony of the sangha. Although a declared Buddhist, he upheld the principle not only of tolerating other faiths but also of giving them honor. He wrote:

> The faiths of others all deserve to be honored for one reason or another. By honoring them, one exalts one's own faith and at the same time performs a service to the faith of others. . . . If a man extols his own faith and disparages another because of devotion to his own and because he wants to glorify it, he seriously injures his own faith.[6]

Asoka promoted respect for parents and teachers, granted amnesty to prisoners, stated that morality is more important than ritual, proscribed the slaughter of animals for use in palace meals, and declared his eagerness to ensure the happiness and well-being of all men (whom he called his "children") in this and any future worlds.

Asoka's service to the Buddhist sangha was that of a very beneficent patron and the settler of internal disputes. He stated that it was his desire that the sangha be unified and last through all time. Thus, he shaped a model that would for many centuries serve kings and governors throughout Asia. Since Śākyamuni had renounced his natural capacity to become a world ruler in order to pursue his spiritual vocation, Asoka has long represented the other option—that of staying within the "secular" world and of translating the truth of the dharma into a social and political reality.[7] Asoka held that self-mastery and the restraint of the passions are important for the establishment of peace and harmony within the political realm; he wrote:

> [I] wish for members of all faiths to live everywhere in my kingdom. For they all seek mastery of the senses and purity of mind.[8]

With the passage of time the sangha expanded and diversified. Initially there had been a rule of perpetual itinerancy; the monks were not only homeless but also intended to live without a fixed residence of any type. Receiving alms from laypersons, their habitations were of utter simplicity—at most a thatched hut or temporary residence in some housing provided by a layperson. Early collections of religious poems by monks and nuns testify to this. At some point within the first centuries, however, it became customary for the monks to remain in one place during the long months of the monsoon rains.[9] Lay patrons provided them with places to stay during these longer periods of time, and it soon became a practice

---

[6] N. A. Nikam and Richard McKeon, ed. and trans., *The Edicts of Asoka* (Chicago: University of Chicago Press, 1959), pp. 51-52.

[7] Bardwell L. Smith, ed., *The Two Wheels of the Dhamma: Essays on the Theravada Tradition in India and Ceylon* (Chambersburg, Pa.: American Academy of Religion, 1972).

[8] Nikam and McKeon, *The Edicts of Asoka*, p. 51.

[9] On this development, see Sukumar Dutt, *Buddhist Monks and Monasteries of India* (London: George Allen & Unwin, 1962), and Ivan Strenski, "On Generalized Exchange and the Domestication of the *Sangha*," *Man*, n.s. Vol. 18, no. 3 (Sept. '83), 463-477.

for one or more monks to remain there year round as "caretakers." Out of this developed the monastery, a place of more or less fixed residence for a number of monks—often in separated cells. Sometimes these were caves cut in rocks and sometimes places built of bricks. The unmistakable fact is that they became more and more elaborate and in some instances were decorated with carvings and paintings as the graphic arts of Buddhism gradually began to develop as well.

As the number of sacred scriptures began to proliferate and as commentaries came to be written, there were some monks who began to excel in scholarly things. With this development, the Buddhist monastery began to assume a role it was to play in many Asian cultures over many centuries, namely, as a center of learning. Monks became masters not only of the Buddhist dharma per se but of virtually every branch of human learning available to them. The network of Buddhist monasteries stretched eventually from India to Japan; they were, in fact, the real universities of Asia and guaranteed a network of intellectual communication among the various cultures that came to adopt Buddhism.

The connection between this and Śākyamuni's enlightenment may, in fact, be closer than it would at first seem. After all, the path of realization that he proclaimed represented a tremendous emphasis upon the human being's potential—not only for a peaceful life but also one that demonstrates a man or woman's mastery of life through intelligence, knowledge, wisdom, and the training of the mind itself. Memorization of vast portions of the scriptural canon was itself often taken to be an indication of spiritual attainment; the mind that could master much was also the mind that demonstrated clarity, depth, and the wisdom to make good choices. Some of these monks in the early tradition no doubt could perform impressive feats of memorization, as monks here and there in the Buddhist world still do today. The emphasis upon the human mind and its powers also is present in the traditional account of Śākyamuni's enlightenment when it is said that a part of this attainment consisted in his new capacity to know the course of all his previous existences. Although Buddhists have always insisted that the touting of one's own knowledge of former lives can easily lead to a very ugly form of spiritual egoism, in the texts that come from India there is a clear supposition that enlightenment entails such a knowledge—even if many humble persons choose to keep that knowledge to themselves. Enlightenment involves the removal of the veils of ignorance that ordinarily hide this part of our own past from ourselves—and in this too Buddhism was unmistakably Indian in its initial intellectual and cultural assumptions. But all of this only underscores the strong emphasis upon the religious significance of enhanced mental powers in Buddhism. It was, therefore, no accident that whole schools of philosophy soon developed and, in fact, proliferated within Buddhism. Monasteries such as the famous one at Nālandā in India housed thousands of monks, so that Chinese pilgrims stopping there could report that within one day a person might attend lectures on an amazingly wide array of different subjects.[10]

---

[10] Arthur Waley, *The Real Tripitaka* (London: George Allen & Unwin, 1952).

PENETRATION INTO EAST ASIA

This development of learning may also help to explain why Buddhism had an immense appeal to peoples outside the borders of India, peoples who before had been only peripherally aware of Indian thought and culture. It may explain why, for instance, it captivated the Chinese, a people otherwise quite content for the most part with the philosophies and religious traditions that were of their own making. For certainly one of the most significant events in human history has been the fact that beginning in the first century C.E., Buddhist ideas began to filter into China, and over the subsequent centuries they were, in fact, to make a very deep impression on the Chinese mind and on Chinese culture.[11] Not only would Indian Buddhists travel to China, but eventually pilgrims from China would visit India, something we know not from the Indians who had almost no interest in writing down historical accounts but from the Chinese who had an immense interest in doing so. The immense canon of holy texts was eventually translated from Sanskrit into the Chinese language so that in some sense a whole new library of religious and philosophical writings came into existence for the Chinese. This was a scholarly enterprise that would be carried on for centuries.[12] The T'ang dynasty (618-907) was one in which Buddhism received lavish royal patronage, schools of Buddhist philosophy flourished, and China was to become a great international cultural magnet, one to which people from all over Asia went for training and learning. As a center of Buddhist education, meditation, and art, China was to be the source from which the Koreans, the Japanese, and the Vietnamese learned how to be Buddhist; moreover, China's Buddhist culture was a stimulus that spurred others on to place the imprint of Buddhism on their own cultures.

Scholars today can debate at length the exact nature of Chinese Buddhism. Some point out that, by being passed through the Chinese mind and Chinese experience, Buddhism lost a good deal of its original Indian character. Also, it had to make its peace eventually with Confucianism and Taoism, the older philosophies of the Chinese.[13] One important way for the Buddhists to prove their respect for the Chinese tradition was by stating that the indigenous philosophies and religions themselves articulated truths that were very valuable and ought not be jettisoned in the people's rush to become Buddhist. However, it is also quite clear that Buddhism fascinated the Chinese, at least in part, because it was different and interesting to them. Buddhist art was at first totally unlike any of the art the Chinese

---

[11] E. Zürcher, *The Buddhist Conquest of China,* 2 vols. (Leiden: E. J. Brill, 1972).

[12] Kenneth K. S. Ch'en, *Buddhism in China: A Historical Survey* (Princeton, N.J.: Princeton University Press, 1964), esp. pp. 365-386.

[13] Tang Yung-tung, "On 'Ko-yi,' The Earliest Method by which Indian Buddhism and Chinese Thought Were Synthesized," in W. R. Inge, ed., *Radhakrishnan: Comparative Studies in Philosophy* (New York, 1950), pp. 276-86, and Arthur E. Link, "The Taoist Antecedents of Tao-an's Pranjñā Ontology," *History of Religions.* Vol. 9, nos. 2, 3 (*Nov. '69 and Feb. '70*), 181-215.

themselves had created earlier; the making of Buddhist images, often gigantic in scale, became an important new ingredient in Chinese culture.

But in the realm of ideas, too, it seems clear that the Chinese were attracted to Indian concepts such as that of *karma,* namely, that all actions lead to inevitable effects upon the person who did them and these effects are either positive or negative. In other words, good deeds bring good rewards and bad deeds bring bad rewards. In addition, even if the reward cannot be seen during the life of a person, there are other lives in which it will certainly be made manifest. Combined as it was with the idea of transmigration through many lives, this novel idea fascinated many Chinese; it offered them a new and interesting way of thinking about life, mortality, what lies beyond death, and the way in which all forms of life are deeply interconnected.

As developed in the forms of Buddhism that reached China, the Buddhist teaching of pratitya-samutpāda was one that claimed that all things in the universe depend upon all other things for existence; nothing can be singled out as having its existence dependent upon itself alone. Even gods, if they exist, are dependent upon other things. This made philosophical sense to many Chinese, and the Buddhists there seem to have relished both this teaching and the earlier-mentioned emphasis upon the mind and its capacities. To people wanting to see the connection between doctrine and the living of daily life, the teaching of pratitya-samutpāda or dependent co-origination seemed to imply that all sentient beings, including wild and domesticated animals, are involved along with us in the same transmigration pattern, one that is shared on a deep level. Therefore, when we kill animals, we violate the lives and sanctity of creatures who very well may have been our human ancestors in some earlier life or lives. To the Chinese, whose Confucian philosophy and religious practice traditionally included a deep respect for all ancestors, this was a striking and impressive new teaching. To many of them, since their cuisine usually included the flesh of many kinds of animals, becoming Buddhist seemed to necessitate becoming vegetarian as well, or at least vegetarian on certain Buddhist days of the calendar or for certain meals. (Although some Indian Buddhists were vegetarians, many others seem not to have pushed the logic quite so far. For them it was the *intention* of an act that was the important thing, and it was not thought unseemly even for monks to eat bits of meat placed in their begging bowls as long as they themselves had not taken the life of the animal involved.) In China the close connection between being Buddhist and being vegetarian led historically to the invention of many rich protein food items from plant sources, especially from the soybean—discoveries that appear to have been made in the kitchens of the large monasteries of medieval China.[14]

Of course, the Buddhism that entered China had already in India undergone

---

[14] K. C. Chang, *Food in Chinese Culture: Anthropological Perspectives* (New Haven, Conn., and London: Yale University Press, 1977). (Check index under "vegetarian foods.")

considerable alteration from the original impulse and simple organization of the earliest sangha. Already mentioned have been moves in the direction of monastic organization and increased philosophical sophistication. Another change of far-reaching importance was the development of what is called the Mahayana or Larger Vehicle. This was a movement that gathered strength in India during the first century B.C.E. and the first century C.E. It grew especially within the *Mahāsanghikas* or adherents of the Great Assembly, one of two sects that resulted from a schism around the time of Asoka; the Mahāsanghikas comprised the more liberal faction and were at that time opposed by the more conservative *Sthaviras* or Elders.[15]

Most of these events had already taken place in India. But it is important to take adequate note of these developments because, otherwise, it is difficult to understand why this form of religious philosophy appealed to the Chinese, a people who otherwise had been totally content to rely only upon indigenous resources. In fact, it is often said that, aside from the impact of Marxism on twentieth-century China, the only other time when the Chinese looked beyond their own borders for intellectual sustenance was during that period when Buddhism was absorbed from India. Since it clearly was Mahayana Buddhism that appealed to the Chinese, its basic structure needs to be described.

The focus of the change to the Mahayana within India can best be represented as a modification of the ideal of enlightenment. Those Buddhists who did not go along with the new Mahayana changes were labeled the *Hinayana* or Smaller Vehicle by their opponents. It was a pejorative term and was intended to suggest that the ideals of this more conservative group were more confined and more limited. The Mahayanists asserted that the others had become too easily satisfied with merely becoming arhats, persons whose whole goal was defined in terms of their own private and individual enlightenment. They charged that the Hinayanists were relatively unconcerned about the fate of others and what would today be called a "social conscience." The Mahayanists claimed that any enlightenment or nirvana enjoyed by an individual in and by himself would not really be enjoyable at all. In their more acerbic comments, they castigated the Hinayanist group as being, at bottom, self-absorbed and even selfish. How, they asked, can the adherents of a philosophy that states that there is no permanent "self" allow themselves to become so concerned only for their own spiritual well-being?

By way of pointing up the contrast, the Mahayanists defined their own goal as that of the bodhisattva.[16] Although this important figure was not, in fact, absent from the ideal pattern of the Small Vehicle group, the Mahayanists wished to make it emphatically their own—or at least a symbol of the difference they sensed between themselves and the others. They made much of the significance of the bod-

---

[15] Edward Conze, *Buddhist Thought in India: Three Phases of Buddhist Philosophy* (Ann Arbor: University of Michigan Press, 1967), pp. 195 ff.

[16] Har Dayal, *The Bodhisattva Doctrine in Buddhist Sanskrit Literature* (London: Kegan Paul, 1932).

hisattva as one who deliberately and intentionally postpones his or her own final enlightenment, choosing instead to remain in samsara, that is, in the painful world of the repeated births and deaths that comprise the fate of the still unenlightened. But the reason that the bodhisattva chooses to remain in samsara is not by necessity but due to his or her wholly altruistic impulse to remain there in order to aid and influence the enlightenment of others still trapped in this sorry round of earthly existences. The Mahayanists held that only a *shared* nirvana, a nirvana in which all distance between self and others as well as all friction between them has been elimi-nated, could be the true one. They held that at bottom the message of the Buddha was one that prescribed a way for men and women to find escape from the prison of the "self" and the attitude of selfishness.

The development of the Mahayana meant, of course, the writing of many new texts expressing this point of view. These texts were originally written in India and in Sanskrit. Although composed sometimes as late as the early centuries C.E., these too were referred to by the Mahayanists as sutras—that is, as texts purported to record words spoken by Śākyamuni during his lifetime. Naturally this exuberant new spawning of sutras could not always guarantee agreement among them, and it required considerable mental agility to try to find ways to solve all these textual and conceptual problems. As the inheritors of these texts, the Chinese felt com-pelled to straighten out the apparent inconsistencies among them; the ingenuity they showed in doing this is itself a fascinating story, although too long to tell here.[17] Probably the most colorful and narratively interesting of these new sutras is the *Saddharma-puṇḍarīka* or Lotus of the Good Dharma, often simply called the Lotus Sutra. Another important group of new Mahayana texts is those called the *Prajñā-pāramitā* or Perfection of Wisdom sutras. These elaborated what the Maha-yanists called *śunyatā* or the doctrine of Emptiness—the principle that *all* things in the cosmos lack the ability to be totally independent or without any need for anything or anyone else. Emptiness is a complex and subtle doctrine, however, and was a principle that gave rise to some of the literary and philosophical gems of the Mayahana. One especially important thinker was an Indian named Nāgārjuna (ca. 150–250 C.E.), whose treatises used an exacting logic to demolish the arguments of any who would assert that something somewhere has its foundation in itself. Nāgārjuna insisted that Emptiness itself, if correctly understood, is dependent too—or, in his words, emptiness too is empty. Śunyatā will be explored further in Chapter 5.

This implied that nirvana and samsara, long thought to be polar opposites and utterly unconnected with each other are, in fact, interconnected and co-dependent. In fact, Nāgārjuna went as far as to write:

There is nothing whatsoever which differentiates the existence-in-flux (sam-sara) from nirvana;

---

[17] Ch'en, *Buddhism in China,* pp. 305 ff.

And there is nothing whatsoever which differentiates nirvana from existence-in-flux (samsara).[18]

This meant that the most holy ideal in Buddhism and the mundane world of pain and evil came to be seen as deeply implicated with one another. This principle gave the Mahayanists a philosophical base for their favorite representation of the bodhisattva as a deeply enlightened being who joyfully stays in samsara so that he or she might work there—they actually often called it "playing there"—for the benefit and salvation of other sentient beings. This concept of the bodhisattva had an immense appeal for many East Asian people. As a concept and powerful symbol, it gave impetus to much of the rich development of Buddhist schools of thought in China. Certainly it was an important basis for the development of that distinctively Chinese form of Buddhism called Ch'an by the Chinese and known in the West by its Japanese name, Zen.

Ch'an was a monastic movement that placed great emphasis upon doing meditation and avoiding abstract thinking. Although it produced its own texts, it detested wordiness. Arthur F. Wright wrote:

> Indeed, Ch'an may be regarded as the reaction of a powerful tradition of Chinese thought against the verbosity, the scholasticism, the tedious logical demonstrations, of the Indian Buddhist texts.[19]

The stress in Ch'an was upon the nonverbal, bodily demonstration of the enlightened mind. Much of this activity took the form of a kind of "playfulness," often childlike, on the part of the monks and sage masters of Ch'an. The literature on this, some of which is looked at in chapters that follow, is rich. Here then was the Indian Mahayana notion of the bodhisattva's playfulness in the world of samsara, but transmuted into the idiom of traditional Chinese patterns and with clear analogues to Taoist notions of the holy man as often a slightly crazy sage.

Another very important type of Buddhism in China was the teaching concerning the Pure Lands presided over by a transcendent Buddhist figure, most frequently that of Amitābha. His Pure Land has been imagined as existing in the West, a "West" that lies beyond this life. The power of this form of Buddhism, not only in China but also in Korea and Japan as well, lay in the way it circumvented the need to project a whole sequence of additional lives and additional deaths before one could hope to attain nirvana. Its appeal to the laity was great, especially because it held out a way of canceling negative karma and promised passage directly to a heavenly mode of existence after a person's present life.

---

[18] Nāgārjuna, "Mūlamadhyamakakārikās," trans. in Frederick J. Streng, *Emptiness: A Study in Religious Meaning* (Nashville, Tenn., and New York: Abingdon Press, 1967), p. 217.

[19] Arthur F. Wright, *Buddhism in Chinese History* (New York: Atheneum, 1968), p. 78.

Many Chinese found it convenient to adhere to more than one school of Buddhism, to move with relative ease from the values found in one to those found in another, and even to combine the teachings of various schools into grander, more embracing syntheses. Criticism from staunch Confucianists—for a whole variety of reasons—made it impossible for Buddhism ever again to regain the power it had had during the period of the T'ang. But vast monasteries of astounding architectural proportions and with very large communities of monks and nuns could still be found in China during the first half of the twentieth century.[20] They also easily accommodated large numbers of lay pilgrims who would stay in these monasteries for important rituals or to practice meditation for a while. The development of the lay movement, however, has been an important aspect of Chinese Buddhist life for the past five hundred years or so.

Buddhism is said to have been introduced to Korea near the end of the fourth century C.E., and there was a very intimate connection between it and the Buddhism of China for many centuries. Patronage by the government, the printing of the entire canon, and impressive works of art characterized the Korean Buddhist community between the eighth and the fourteenth centuries. However, with the founding of a new dynasty in 1392, one that was based on strict adherence to Confucian norms, Korean Buddhism began to be suppressed. As Buddhists were forced to relinquish their urban temples, the strength of their movement shifted to the mountain monasteries. These became places to which many lay Buddhists went for religious pilgrimage over the subsequent centuries. Discipline among the monks and nuns of these mountain temples remained strict, and in the twentieth century, Korean Buddhism has been undergoing a revival and is beginning to be seen more and more in the cities once again.[21]

The Japanese took to Buddhism quite rapidly—especially because of the immense prestige it had in China and Korea. Officially introduced by Korean kings who sent sutras and images to the Japanese court in the sixth century C.E., socially Buddhism remained largely an aristocratic movement for some centuries—although great scholar-monks such as Kūkai (774-835) and Saicho (766-822) formed schools of teaching that continue even to the present. Then in the twelfth and thirteenth centuries, a series of charismatic Buddhist leaders—of the Pure Land schools, of the Zen schools, and Nichiren (1222-1282), whose schools bear his name—made Buddhism intelligible and important to the masses. These men are often referred to as the great teachers of the Kamakura era (1192-1338); they left an indelible stamp on Japanese Buddhism, one that remains today. During all of Japan's medieval period, the connection between Mahayana Buddhism and literature, especially

---

[20] J. Prip-Møller, *Chinese Buddhist Monasteries* (London: Oxford University Press, 1937), and Holmes Welch, *The Practice of Chinese Buddhism, 1900-1950* (Cambridge, Mass.: Harvard University Press, 1967).

[21] Heinrich Dumoulin, "Contemporary Buddhism in Korea," in H. Dumoulin, ed., *Buddhism in the Modern World* (New York: Macmillan, 1976), pp. 202-214.

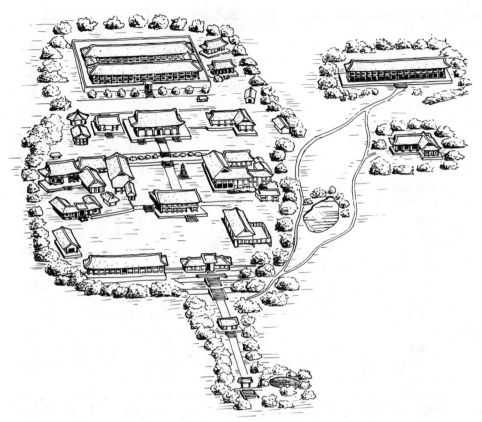

Haein-sa Monastery, Korea

poetry, was an intimate one.[22] Zen also became a powerful force in Japanese political and cultural life during this same period.[23] Then during the Tokugawa period (1600–1868), all Japanese households were required to have membership in Buddhist parishes and the temples were part of the strict social control exercised by the shoguns, a move that in many ways robbed the Buddhist schools of "nearly all spiritual freedom."[24] Nevertheless, Japanese Buddhism has always been able to coexist quite comfortably with the indigenous Shinto religion and dominated the intellectual life of the country for well over a thousand years. Some of its forms,

---

[22] William R. LaFleur, *The Karma of Words: Buddhism and the Literary Arts in Medieval Japan* (Berkeley, Los Angeles, and London: University of California Press, 1983).

[23] Martin Collcutt, *Five Mountains: The Rinzai Zen Monastic Institution in Medieval Japan* (Cambridge, Mass., and London: Harvard University Press, 1981).

[24] Joseph M. Kitagawa, "The Buddhist Transformation in Japan," *History of Religions,* Vol. 4, no. 2 (1965), p. 328; see also his *Religion in Japanese History* (New York and London: Columbia University Press, 1966).

especially those of Zen and Nichiren, have begun to make some impact on the West, as well, in our century. In addition during the modern period, Japanese thinkers, some of them deeply influenced by their Mahayana tradition, have begun to be engaged in dialogue with Christian theologians and Western philosophers.

THE THERAVADA

Although it was not the only one in Buddhist history, the split between the Mahā-sanghikas and the Sthaviras was one that had far-reaching consequences. We have seen how the former were the primary matrix out of which developed the Mahayana, the kind of Buddhism that largely spread north and east from India. The Sthavira spawned a number of schools and underwent further divisions and separations. The most important of these, however, is undoubtedly the school called the Theravada, a term chosen to refer to the Path followed by the Elders and thereby one that stresses the essentially conservative orientation of this school. Its adherents identify themselves as remaining true to the teachings and practices of the earliest sangha. It has always been especially important within this school to have monks who are properly ordained and live their lives in the traditional manner. It is this school that spread primarily to Sri Lanka, Burma, Thailand, Laos, and Cambodia. It possesses its own canon of scriptures in the Pali language, a vernacular language of Western India related to Sanskrit but treasured especially by the Theravadins because there has been some supposition that it might even have been the language originally used by Śākyamuni. This canon is of tremendous importance because of its antiquity—written down in the second century B.C.E.—and because, throughout the centuries, Pali has served the Theravada school as a special, ecclesiastical language somewhat like "Church Latin" has served in Europe.

Asoka is said to have sent a mission of Buddhists to Sri Lanka around the year 247 B.C.E., and it appears that the Sinhalese had generally accepted the Buddhist dharma within one hundred years of that date. The Asokan model has been important for the island nation; the sangha there has generally benefited from patronage and a long tradition of kings and rulers deeply committed to protecting Buddhism and receiving the sangha's support in return.[25] In Sri Lanka it is clear that Buddhism is the state religion, even though this often creates difficulties for the Hindu minority on the island. The majority feels that the existence of a strong sangha there has much to do with their national identity. Long occupation by Europeans between 1505 and 1948—first the Portuguese, then the Dutch, and finally the British—put a considerable strain on the sangha. In the latter half of the twentieth century, however, Buddhism in Sri Lanka seemed to recover its vitality. The Sri Lankans are generally pleased to have had an important historical role in the preser-

---

[25] Bardwell L. Smith, "The Ideal Social Order as Portrayed in the Chronicles of Ceylon," in Smith, ed., *Religion and Legitimation of Power in Sri Lanka* (Chambersburg, Pa.: Anima Books, 1978), pp. 48–72.

vation of Theravada Buddhism for more than two thousand years. Among the many great scholar monks there the most famous was Buddhaghosa (late fourth to early fifth centuries C.E.), an Indian who resided in Sri Lanka and wrote *The Path of Purity,* a classic treatise on doctrine, on how to interpret the sutras, and on meditative practices in the Theravada tradition.

Burma, like Sri Lanka, is said to have received Buddhism due to Asoka's decision to send a mission there; since then its role in the Burmese people's self-definition of their own nationhood has been clear and strong. Although Mahayana forms from China and Hinduism from India made inroads into Burmese life at some points in history, the Burmese have been and remain strongly committed to the Theravada sangha. One specially glorious phase of this history was during the Pagān kingdom (849–1287), a period during which royal favor, a capital city with thousands of temples and stupas, and a vibrant intellectual life made Pagān perhaps the most important center of Buddhist culture in the world.[26] In 1065 monks were even sent from there to Sri Lanka to reestablish the purity of the Theravada tradition on that island. Attacked by the Mongols in 1287, Pagān as a city was destroyed, but Theravada was resilient. Even British rule for centuries only hardened the Burmese people's commitment to be a Buddhist nation.

Thailand too has a strong Theravada tradition—although its sangha is younger than those of Burma and Sri Lanka. As part of the Khmer empire it received extensive cultural influence from India by the fifth century C.E. This was also an ecclectic influence: a Hindu royal cult was present as were forms of the Mahayana. The Khmer empire eventually came apart and so, in the twelfth and thirteenth centuries, Theravada monks from Burma made their strong and lasting impact on Thai culture. Unlike the other nations of south and southeast Asia, Thailand was not colonized by Europeans. Perhaps one of its most impressive aspects is its aesthetic aspect; many of its temples—with stunning flamelike designs on the roofs and portals with filigree, and with beautiful bronze and gold images of Buddha—are renowned throughout the world. Here too Theravada has been virtually the religion of the state.

Cambodia, Laos, portions of Vietnam, and also Indonesia were all influenced by Indian culture. This included both Buddhist and Hindu influences so that the religious life of the people in these countries historically appeared to be somewhat "syncretistic." This does not mean that Buddhist monks adopted Hindu ways or that brahmins practiced Buddhism; it simply means that for the lay population of these lands, it was not thought unseemly to pay attention to both the Hindu cult and the Buddhist monks located in their communities. Much of Vietnam received mostly Mahayana influences from its northern neighbor, China, but the Buddhism of these southeast Asian nations included both Theravada and Mahayana forms. Architectural achievement on a grand scale was part of this: most notable are the old royal cities of Cambodia and the great monument of Barabadur on the island

---

[26] George H. Luce, *Old Burma—Early Pagān,* 3 vols. (Locust Valley, N.Y.: J. J. Augustin, 1969–70).

of Java, a mountain of stone made by the islanders that lets those who pilgrimage up it have a sense of literally moving up out of the world of samsara and into that of nirvana.[27] The actual condition of the Buddhist sanghas in Cambodia, Laos, and Vietnam remains largely unknown due to the changed political situation in those countries. We know more about Indonesia where some centuries ago syncretism weakened the specificity of the Buddhist dharma and where, by the end of the fourteenth century, Islam had converted most of the islands' population.

EXPANSION NORTHWARD AND TO THE "WEST"

Already by the second century B.C.E. Buddhism had gained a strong foothold in northwestern India, the culture of which at that time combined Greek influences from the West with Indian ones from the south and east. Especially in Gandhāra in what today is Afghanistan, a vibrant Greco-Buddhist culture came into existence, and the first iconographic representations of the Buddha—probably in the first century B.C.E.—show remarkable influences from classical Greek sculpture. These images, with the perceptible body form under a thin veil of draped robes, have sometimes been called the "Indian Apollo." This rich artistic development was encouraged by the kings of that area, wealthy men who were also in the process of building powerful city-states that were to be the nodal points in the centuries-long transportation of merchandise, works of art, Buddhist learning, and general knowledge across the heart of central Asia.

This was the development of the famed Silk Road, a communication and transportation network on land that was Asia's equivalent of the Mediterranean Sea. For centuries it was traversed by traders' caravans and Buddhist pilgrims all the way from the Mediterranean centers of Greek civilization, across ancient Persia and central Asia, and right into the capital cities of China. Moreover, the testimony of artifacts in an eighth-century Japanese storehouse in Nara, a city built under pervasive Buddhist influence, shows that in some sense this celebrated and culturally important Silk Road even had a Far Eastern extension over water to the Japanese islands; items in the storehouse in Nara came from as far away as Persia.[28] Today the Buddhist-influenced civilization along much of this route is gone, having succumbed in part to the encroaching desert but also having been destroyed by zealous devotees of Islam in the tenth century. Not only have temples, scriptures, and precious art disappeared, but also have whole monasteries and the communities inside them as well.

Before this great loss, however, the Silk Road created an ecumenical, unusually "open" age in world history. It was an era when important Chinese Buddhists

---

[27] Paul Mus, *Barabadur* (Hanoi, 1935; in French); Philip Rawson, *The Art of Southeast Asia* (New York and Washington, D.C.: Frederick A. Praeger, 1967).

[28] Ryoichi Hayashi, *The Silk Road and the Shosoin,* trans. by Robert Ricketts (New York and Tokyo: Weatherhill/Heibonsha, 1975).

Hsüan-tsang Carrying Sutras

went on pilgrimage to India and left records of what they did and saw. Perhaps the most famous of these is Hsüan-tsang (602–664), who traveled by land to India and then stayed there for nearly twenty years in order to acquire Buddhist scriptures that he then took back to China. He wrote an account of his experiences, entitled *Journey to the West,* an incomparable source of information about much of Asia during that period of remarkable cultural exchange. Hsüan-tsang became a hero to the Chinese and a humorous, picaresque novel based in part on his adventures has delighted the Chinese for centuries.[29] Another testimony to that remarkable era is the group of caves at Tun-huang on the edge of western China. These are treasure houses of Buddhist art, sutras, and popular fiction; they somehow escaped the iconoclasm of Islam. The excavation of these caves during the twentieth century has proven it to be one of the greatest archeological "finds" of modern times. What has been found there is still the subject of intense and fascinating research.

During some of this development, the mountain people of Tibet remained relatively unaffected, bypassed to the north by the Silk Road and still not impacted greatly by the culture of India to the south. In the early seventh century C.E., however, this began to change when King Songtsen Gampo (d. 649) introduced Buddhism to Tibet, at least according to tradition. Actually, Tibet has had many centuries of intimate contact with both India and China, disproving Westerners' old, romantic notions of Tibet as a Shangri-la locked forever behind her mountains. Although recent research has shown that Ch'an Buddhism from China

---

[29] Anthony C. Yu, trans., *The Journey to the West,* 4 vols. (Chicago: University of Chicago Press, 1977–83).

entered Tibet at a relatively early date,[30] for the most part the Tibetans regarded their two powerful neighbors quite differently. R. A. Stein states that in the Tibetans' eyes "India has always been the land of religion whereas the land of secular laws has been China."[31] This is a preference that may even be reflected in the result of a celebrated debate—maybe better called a "verbal duel"—sponsored by a Tibetan king between 792 and 794. On that occasion, the path of "gradual enlightenment" or the attainment of the Buddhist goal along a step-by-step path was defended by Indian monks in Tibet, whereas the position of "sudden enlightenment" or attainment all at one time was argued by Chinese monks of the Ch'an tradition. Although accounts differ, it is claimed that the king decided things in favor of the Indians and even required that the Chinese leave the country.[32] The Buddhism of Mongolia was largely Tibetan in its origin, and during the period when the Manchus ruled China itself (1644-1911), it was really a Tibetan form of Buddhism, mediated by way of Mongolian peoples, that held sway in the Chinese court.

But the Buddhism borrowed early from India by the Tibetans was not exactly of the kind we have depicted up to this point in our narrative. In fact, since the arrival of Buddhism into Tibet was at a relatively late date, the form of Buddhism flourishing in India at the time when the Tibetans borrowed most heavily, was of the type called *tantra,* a form of religious expression that is fond of "direct, immediate, and bodily union between a practitioner and his goal."[33] The tantric development in India began around the eighth century and influenced almost every form of religious life. Buddhist tantra, however, was based on the principle of the *Prajñā-pāramitā* according to which the highest Wisdom (*prajñā*) ought to be "at play" with the most perfect form of Skill-in-application (*upāya*). Prajñā and upāya should, in fact, be in a condition of the most perfect union. Moreover, according to tantra, the most perfect symbol of "perfect union" and of being "at play" is that of blissful sexual union. The imagery, art, and language forms of tantra, even of Buddhist tantra, therefore, usually are often sexually explicit. But it is important to remember that this tantra also represented an extension of the doctrine of śunyatā or Emptiness; therefore, it involved use of the subtle logic of the great Indian Buddhist philosopher Nāgārjuna. Nāgārjuna's philosophy, in fact, has always been revered highly within the Tibetan sangha, and its points were for centuries debated there with great sophistication.

The Tibetans have been very devout Buddhists; at some points in history fully a third of the adult male population of Tibet was comprised of monks. Yet tantra, they discovered, could move in very different directions, and the precise

---

[30] Jeffrey Broughton, "Early Ch'an Schools in Tibet," in Robert M. Gimello and Peter N. Gregory, eds., *Studies in Ch'an and Hua-yen* (Honolulu: University of Hawaii Press, 1983), pp. 1-68.

[31] R. A. Stein, *Tibetan Civilization,* trans. by J. E. Stapleton Driver (Stanford, Calif.: Stanford University Press, 1972), p. 53.

[32] Stein, *Tibetan Civilization,* p. 68.

[33] Kinsley, *Hinduism,* pp. 19-20.

location of the Middle Path was not always agreed upon or easy to determine for the Tibetans. On the one hand, many monks, even highly placed ones, married and sometimes understood their "attainment" to be something that even permitted what others might consider debauchery; they also dabbled in the politics of Tibet and Tibet's relationships with her Chinese and Mongolian neighbors. On the other hand, some monks insisted that the tantric way is philosophical and symbolic; it should not make licentious ways legitimate. Judging that the relaxation of the sangha's rules had gone too far, Tsongkha-pa (1357–1419) carried out a reform and founded a new order of monks that, though based on Nāgārjuna's Mahayana articulation of Emptiness, insisted upon strict monastic discipline and a code of morality virtually as strict as that used in the Theravada tradition. This new order later gave rise to the tradition of the Dalai Lama, a uniquely Tibetan institution according to which it is held that Avalokiteśvara, the celestial Bodhisattva of Compassion, is reincarnated again and again in special persons who as infants are located by a process of divination and then brought up to be not only the highest spiritual but also the temporal ruler of Tibet. The fourteenth Dalai Lama (1935–   ) left Tibet, along with approximately 100,000 of his countrymen and 10,000 monks after the Chinese annexed Tibet into China in 1959. Since that time, much of the leadership of Tibetan Buddhism has lived in exile in India and various locations in Europe and America.

In India, Buddhism quite rapidly declined after the efflorescence of tantra—perhaps because it had gotten out of touch with the ordinary religious needs of village people in that largely agricultural land. Islam's growth in India brought about Buddhism's final demise; the great monastery at Nālandā, for instance, was burned down in 1198 and many of its monks died. Likewise, the state of Buddhism in China and certain countries of Southeast Asia is uncertain today as well. Sri Lanka, Burma, and Thailand, of course, appear to remain deeply committed to continued maintenance of their rich Theravada traditions. Japanese Buddhism often gives a confusing picture to Westerners—sometimes seeming still to have deep roots in the culture, arts, and lives of people and sometimes seeming ready to admit to being, in fact, greatly diminished due to the industrialization of Japan and the strong impact of Western cultural forms there. Although Japanese opinion on this question is divided, there are some Japanese that have even suggested, half in jest no doubt, that Japan may some day have to "reimport" Buddhism, including Zen, from the West. Modern scholarship on the texts and history of Buddhism began in Europe, although in the twentieth century Japanese scholarship on Buddhist texts and history has become the strongest in the world. It is worth noting that much of the modern West's own scholarship on Buddhism during the late nineteenth and twentieth centuries indirectly contributed to the Buddhist revivals that have taken place in some of the nations of Asia. The translation of sutras and other texts into various Western languages as well as the reconstruction of the history of Buddhism is an ongoing project. The tireless lecturing and writing of D. T. Suzuki (1870–1966) in the West are said to have made "Zen" into an English word. In addition various Buddhist communities and even the beginnings of a sangha of monks and nuns has come into being in Europe and America during the twentieth century.

THE GREAT DEATH IN A MUD VILLAGE

At seventy-nine years of age Śākyamuni, the Buddha, was still an itinerant teacher in India, walking from town to town and stopping for food and shelter at the homes of persons who had become lay members of his growing community of disciples. Among these laymen there was a great eagerness to provide hospitality for the Buddha, not only because such hospitality was considered a great virtue by Indians in general but also because it gave these Buddhists a chance to practice the virtue of giving or *dāna*—a word that, incidentally, is a distant relative of the English word "donation." This virtue was considered the first step on the road to enlightenment. Such hospitality also gave such laypersons an opportunity to be close to the man they most admired in all the world.

It had now been at least forty-five years since that night when Śākyamuni, as a man determined to stay rooted in the lotus posture doing meditation until his goal was realized, had attained enlightenment under a tree outside the city of Bodh Gaya. This, the nirvana that came after a night of the most intense kind of struggle, was the foundation for all he taught during the subsequent decades of his life. It was this transformation that made it possible for people to refer to him as the Buddha or Enlightened One.

But now he was almost eighty, not only old but also weary. Since everything terrifying about death had already been met and overcome by him on the night of his great enlightenment, dying was now something he could meet with perfect tranquility of mind. Knowing that he would never return to Vaiśālī, the one city where he had spent much time, he stopped over in a mango grove during his journey. A smith named Chunda heard that the Buddha was nearby and took this opportunity to invite him and his disciples to his home for a meal the next day. He went and issued an invitation. By silence, the sign of consent, Śākyamuni accepted Chunda's offer of hospitality.

Being a smith, Chunda was not of high caste in India, although this did not necessarily mean that he was poor. In any case he prepared the best meal he could. It was comprised of sweet rice, cakes, and some additional foodstuff that we today cannot easily identify. Yet this, the mysterious item on the menu, turns out to have been the one of critical importance for the events of the next day. It, therefore, needs some explanation. It was a dish that the texts call *sūkara-maddhava,* and it clearly seems to have something to do with pigs. (The first syllable of this phrase is probably linked by the long ancestral lines of the Indo-European language family to the Latin word "sus," an Old English word "su," and even, perhaps, our modern English word "sow.") It is important to note that the exact meaning of this word has troubled Buddhists for a long time and has been a reason for much disagreement among modern scholars as well. The reasons for this are interesting.

The problem is that the word sūkara-maddhava occurs only once in all of Indian literature; there is, thus, no place other than this one reference to make a check on its exact meaning. Some say it must have meant the meat of a pig and that Śākyamuni ate contaminated pork as part of his last meal. Theravada Buddhists have often accepted this explanation since their rules, although very strict in other ways, did not prohibit a monk from accepting and eating animal meat that was included among other things received from laypersons as a food offering, as long as the animal had not been butchered especially for the monk's food. The Theravada code of rules did not make any blanket statement that a monk must be vegetarian. (This Theravada code, incidentally, was also adopted by many Tibetans who, otherwise, were usually Mahayanist in their doctrines. This had made it allowable for Tibetan Buddhists, where the ecology of mountain life makes being vegetarian much more difficult than in India, to eat meat.[34]) The point is that most Theravadins have not been shocked by the suggestion that even Śākyamuni ate pork at Chunda's residence.

To most Mahayanists, however, this explanation seemed outrageous. The reason, in brief, was that Mahayanists were strongly convinced that all sentient beings have Buddha-nature or the potential for becoming Buddhas. They—and especially the many Chinese who became Buddhists—could vividly imagine that creatures encountered as animals in this life may during some other life have been members of our human family, perhaps even our parents or ancestors. As a result, the Mahayana code was very specific and exact on this point: monks were strictly forbidden to eat animal flesh.[35] Laypersons, too, often observed this. Therefore, it became impossible for them to envision the possibility of Śākyamuni eating the meat of a pig.

The problem, then, for the Mahayanists was what sūkara-maddhava could possibly mean, since it clearly had something to do with pigs. They worked their way around this problem by taking this food to have been some kind of mushroom that pigs either eat or unearth with their snouts. The early translations of this text, *The Sutra of the Great Decease [Passing]*, into English also assume that the Buddha was a strict vegetarian; it rendered Chunda's special dish as "truffles." The question, however, has remained far from settled[36] and scholars will continue to discuss it for some time.

But in any case, whatever kind of food it was, it was clearly toxic. And when he saw this food that Chunda had prepared, Śākyamuni, by means of the extraordinary clairvoyance that was his, is said to have been able to detect the presence of

---

[34] D. Seyfort Ruegg, "Ahimsā and Vegetarianism in the History of Buddhism," in Somaratna Balasooriya and others, eds., *Buddhist Studies in Honor of Walpola Rahula* (London: Gordon Fraser, and Sri Lanka: Vimamsa, 1980), p. 234.

[35] Ibid., pp. 237–238; also Arthur Waley, "Did Buddha Die of Eating Pork?" *Melanges chinois et bouddhiques,* Vol. 1 (1931–32), 343–354.

[36] R. Gordon Wasson, "The Last Meal of the Buddha," *Journal of the American Oriental Society,* Vol. 102, no. 4 (October–December 1982), 591–603.

something deadly in it. Before the meal began, he addressed his host and asked him to divide the food in a very unusual way:

> As for the sūkara-maddhava which you have prepared, Chunda, I ask that you serve it to me alone. And as for what I cannot consume, such leftovers I would like to have you bury in a hole in the ground. However, the other food such as the sweet rice and cakes may be fed to my brothers, the fellow-monks who are here with me today.[37]

It was a puzzling request, but Chunda did exactly as the Buddha had asked him to do. Then, knowing full well what would happen, Śākyamuni ate the food that was poisonous. The account goes on to say that

> there then fell upon the Buddha a terrible sickness, the disease of dysentery and sharp pains afflicted him even to the point of threatening his life. But the Buddha, keeping his concentration of mind and self-possessed, bore this sickness without complaint.[38]

He did not die at once because there still remained a number of things he wished to do. He decided first to travel with his company to a nearby village by the name of Kusinagara, a place even farther into the countryside and away from urban power and wealth. When he arrived there he lay down on his right side in a grove between two trees; one leg was resting on the other and his mind was concentrated and peaceful. It is said that at that time the trees burst into bloom even though it was not the season for them to do so. This has usually been regarded as appropriate for someone whose biography often includes special interaction between himself and the natural world, including one occasion when by the power of his mind alone he tamed a wild, rampaging elephant.

In spite of this, Ānanda, one of his chief disciples, wondered aloud why his master had chosen to die in such an out-of-the-way and insignificant town. To the Buddha he said:

> Let the exalted One not die in this little village where things are put together out of twigs and mud, one in the middle of the jungle and only part of what is only a branch township. Master, let us go to one of the big cities where there are wealthy patrons and followers who will pay full honor and reverence your remains.[39]

---

[37] This is from "The Book of the Great Decease" (*Mahā Parinibbāna Suttanta*) in *Dialogues of the Buddha* Translated from the Pali by T. W. and C. A. F. Rhys Davids (Part II) (London: Henry Frowde, Oxford University Press, 1910), p. 138. Here and in following quotations the language has been slightly modernized.

[38] *Dialogues,* p. 138.

[39] *Dialogues,* p. 161.

The response of the Buddha was one that depended upon the extraordinary knowledge of the past that in India has always been identified with holy sages and enlightened men. He told Ānanda that this town of mud and twigs called Kushinagara had, in fact, an illustrious history; ages before it had been the royal city of a great and righteous king, a man properly referred to as a king of kings. With this explanation, Ānanda understood his master's choice.

Then the Buddha told his disciples to leave the grove and go to tell the people of the village that he was dying. "Otherwise," he said, "they will later reproach themselves for not having come out here to the grove to be with me during my final hours." So they went out as instructed. And the people came. They came, in fact, in droves from all over. And because there was not time enough for each of them as individuals to pay their last respects to him, they were arranged in family groups and in this fashion bowed together and gave him their final greeting. To a skeptic by the name of Subhadda, he gave a detailed exposition of his teaching—so thorough, in fact, that the man was totally convinced and became, therefore, the last person to make the decision to enter the course of the Middle Path having listened to the direct teachings of Śākyamuni himself.

At this point the Buddha turned again to the inner circle of his disciples, those who had lived a basically wandering life with him for many years. He asked if any of them had any misgivings or doubts. "Otherwise," he said, "you might later reproach yourselves for not having raised questions and problems while still face-to-face with me." He asked them three times, but their continued silence indicated that there were no more problems remaining in their minds. Ānanda, as spokesperson, proclaimed: "How wonderful it is, Master! There is not one in our assembly that has any doubts concerning the Buddha, the teachings, the path, or the method." With this it seems that the inner circle of the sangha or community was now as ready to accept his death as was the Buddha himself.

Finally he spoke his last words, two sentences that have for centuries been lodged in the collective memory of the Buddhist community. The first was:

Decay is inherent in all composite things.[40]

It was a simple and firm declaration that there are no exceptions to the rule of impermanence. There is nothing that is not in some way or another put together, that is, a composition made out of still other elements. And since all things are such compositions, all things eventually come apart. The rule is universal, without exceptions. Even Buddhas pass away. The only difference is that an enlightened one dies with such tranquility and strength of mind that his or her death or dissolution cannot be thought of in negative or in pessimistic terms. Therefore, the second sentence from the Buddha's mouth on his deathbed was a simple command that his disciples also bend every effort to pursue the same goal. This is one of the most

---

[40] *Dialogues*, p. 173.

important statements in the Buddhist scriptures, one considered an encapsulation of the dharma discovered and taught by Śākyamuni. He said:

Work out your own realization with diligence![41]

Each disciple was thus challenged to devote all available intelligence and energy to the discovery of a similar tranquility, knowledge, and strength.

Then came his actual passing, a series of raptures through which he progressed. Since he was what Buddhists believe to have been an unparalleled master of the ways of yogic meditation, he ended his life by a perfectly controlled sequence of steps in the range of the mind's powers. Part of the lengthy description of this is as follows:

> Rising out of the fourth stage of rapture, he entered into that state of mind to which the infinity of space alone is present. And passing out of the mere consciousness of the infinity of space, he entered into the state of mind to which the infinity of thought is alone present. [From there] . . . he passed into a state where nothing at all was especially present. [From there] . . . he passed into a state between consciousness and unconsciousness. . . . Then all consciousness . . . had passed away.[42]

But even now he was not yet dead. As though having perfect control of things even within the realm of the unconscious, he reopened the doors to the various levels of consciousness once again. It was as though he could open and close these at will and perform a passage that was perfectly unimpeded. At the end, he even reversed his reversal. It was a mental and spiritual virtuosity that his disciples noted and considered unmatched among men. And then came the final move, a passing that was really simple:

> And passing out of the third stage he entered into the fourth stage of rapture. And passing out of the last stage of rapture, he immediately expired.[43]

Tradition has it that the earth itself reacted. There was a tremendous earthquake and a loud crack of thunder that rolled across the sky. Among the larger company of his followers, there were two different reactions. Some, said to be those still not free from their passions, cried out, wept, and fell down to the ground in their sorrow. "The light," they lamented, "has gone out of our world!" But others, those said to be free from their passions, were completely composed. They recollected the Buddha's final words, his statement that all things undergo change and dissolution. But this was not a matter of merely accepting it stoically or with resignation.

---

[41] *Dialogues,* p. 173.

[42] *Dialogues,* pp. 173–174.

[43] *Dialogues,* p. 175.

On the contrary, they viewed the tranquility of this death as another indication of the Buddha's deep enlightenment. This passing was all of one piece with the nirvana of forty-five years earlier; they, therefore, called this event his *parinirvāṇa,* or the perfected nirvana. It was the culmination of his release.

The account goes on to say that, while his body lay covered with flowers and perfumes in the grove of trees, the people of that place paid reverence both to his life and to his passing with music, hymns, and dancing. They continued this for six days. Then on the seventh they planned his cremation. It seemed only fitting to give him a funeral befitting a king of kings, so they wrapped him in a thousand layers of cloth and built a pyre out of many kinds of perfumed oil.

Each disciple now paid final homage. Then the body is said to have ignited spontaneously and to have burned in a most unusual way. It gave off neither soot nor ash, burning as if it were pure oil or ghee, the clarified butter so prized in India. Finally only *śarīra,* the refined earthly residue of an enlightened one, remained when the fire extinguished itself. These were, naturally, very precious to his disciples. They were distributed to laypersons among his followers and were carried off to many places in the land. Eventually some were carried far beyond India, to locations in China, Southeast Asia, Tibet, Korea, and Japan. These relics were all that remained of the body of the Buddha, and it quickly became a custom for pious people to house these precious remains in the kind of reliquary called a stupa. These relics and stupas symbolized and accompanied the expansion of the Buddhist community far beyond the village of Kusinagara. But it had, remarkably, been the people of this mere "twig-and-mud" village that had been privileged to be present at this unparalleled event in Buddhist history, the fulfillment of the nirvana of Śākyamuni, the Buddha.

Modern estimates place the date of this passing at approximately 480 B.C.E. It was an event that was destined to become a central one on the Buddhist yearly calendar and one celebrated in Buddhist cultures as something festive rather than morbid. It inspired numberless people to emulate something of the character of Śākyamuni's life so that they too might have tranquility and ease in their dying. Artists and poets, likewise, took it as the theme and inspiration for painting and for verse, often capturing the death as one that was not private and alone but in the midst of an admiring community, witnessed by nature and the cosmos as a whole. A little village in the middle of the jungle had been the location of a most profound event.

ZEN'S FIRST PATRIARCH: LEGEND AND HISTORY

Good historical analysis tries to sift through things so as to separate what seem to be the facts from other things that might only be legend or lore. But another thing that must be done by the historian is to recognize that legends, even though they may not have much fact behind them, often come to have a great historical role once they get to be believed by people and are widely accepted as important. The historian, therefore, even when he finds the legend hard to believe, has to try to explain why it arose in the first place, got to be believed for such a long time, and still continues to retain a certain charm or power.

The figure of Bodhidharma is like that. As for hard facts we really know nothing about him, although some scholars claim to see proof that he was an Indian monk, that he sailed to China in the fifth century c.e., and that he was an interpreter of the *Lankāvatāra Sūtra*,[44] an important Mahayana text that many consider to have been the basis for that form of Buddhism that the Chinese call Ch'an, the Koreans call Son, and the Japanese and Westerners call Zen.

On these very scanty facts a rich and powerful legend is based—and it is a legend that had great historical importance. Here we will tell the narrative of the legend and comment on its role in Buddhist history. The lore has it that Bodhidharma, whose name is a compound of "enlightenment" (*bodh*) and dharma, traveled intentionally to China with the sole purpose of desiring to bring Zen east to the Chinese. (Note that this was about one thousand years after Śākyamuni had lived and already about five hundred years since Buddhism had been introduced to China.) The bringing of Zen was supposed to be something very special indeed. But upon his arrival in China, Bodhidharma did not set about propagating his teaching in the ordinary and expected way by gathering crowds who might listen to him and convincing his audience concerning the truth of what he was saying. Instead, almost immediately upon his arrival in China, he did something quite bizarre; he went into a cave in the mountains and sat facing the wall there for nine years.

But he first had a chat with the emperor, namely, Emperor Wu of the Liang dynasty (reigned 502-549). Emperor Wu was someone special because his devotion to Buddhism is a well-established fact; we know from reliable sources that he supported the sangha lavishly, built a series of magnificent temples, and convened large vegetarian feasts for the monks and laity. He himself wrote commentaries on Buddhist texts. Emperor Wu is also well known for his practice of going off to monasteries for retreats, having prearranged for his highest ministers of state to show up later at these monasteries in order to fetch him to return to the capital and perform his duties as emperor again. In the process they paid large sums as "ransom" to the sangha for the return of their ruler. All this was a rather unusual way in which the pious emperor lavished his wealth on the Buddhist sangha.

The legend concerning the meeting between Emperor Wu and Bodhidharma, however, tells that the emperor, having heard that a famous Indian holy man was in his realm, invited him to his palace. Then, pointing to some of his own good deeds in support of Buddhism—and quite possibly expecting some praise for having performed them—the emperor asked the monk if there were merit in such charity. "No! No merit at all!" was the terse and direct answer of the Indian, a response

---

[44] The Lankāvatāra Sūtra, trans. by Daisetz Teitara Suzuki (Boulder, Colo.: Prajña Press, 1978). But see especially Bernard Faure, "Bodhidharma as Textual and Religious Paradigm," *History of Religions* 25:3 (Feb. 1986), pp. 187-198.

that itself anticipated the laconic kind of speech much preferred in Zen. The narrative goes on to say that with this brief encounter Bodhidharma left, went to his cave in a mountain in northern China, and began his nine years of wall gazing. The direct, less than gentle way in which the Zen master put the emperor in his place, even a pious and beneficent one, is much relished in the Zen tradition.

The nine years of solitary wall gazing is the centerpiece of the lore about Bodhidharma. Supposedly he was already sixty years old when he arrived in China. Having crossed the sea and having come to a foreign country thought to be desperately in need of gaining an understanding of the "true" form of Buddhism, he literally buries himself now in a mountain. But he buries himself in order to do meditation. Therefore, he really throws himself into intentional obscurity in order to practice precisely what he would otherwise wish to preach. Once on Chinese soil he *does* what he wants the Chinese to understand. He teaches not by words that might lead to texts full of verbosity but by direct action and example.

The charm and power of the legend lie in this. He seems to have been ready to let his whole mission abort and his secret die with him in the cave rather than force it on others if they appeared to be not yet hungry for it. So he waited . . . and waited for a total of nine years until some Chinese somewhere was burning with a desire to learn this Indian master's secret. That person was a Chinese monk named Hui-k'o, who is reputed to have lived for 108 years (487–595). On the occasion of importance he sought out Bodhidharma. In finding the Indian in his cave he also found that the master's legs had atrophied and he had cut off his own eyelids so that his eyes would not close in sleep and thereby stop the meditation that he wanted to carry out without interruption. The old Indian holy man was, to say the least, also an extraordinary ascetic.

At this point the narrative takes up a typical, almost paradigmatic Zen motif, namely, the master's repeated refusal to take on the student even when the latter begs and pleads with him. In this the mettle of the potential disciple is tested. (Even today some prospective Zen monks in Japan are required to sit in the entry hall of temples for many days before they are permitted to go inside.) The aspirant must prove his unflagging intention to pursue the Zen course against all odds. Certainly Hui-k'o did so. The story has it that he stood outside in the snow until it covered his legs. But he did much more than that. When Bodhidharma repeatedly refused to take him on as his understudy, the intrepid Chinese, not to be outdone by the asceticism of the Indian, demonstrated his sincerity by cutting off his own arm and presenting it to Bodhidharma as a concrete token of the steadfast nature of his purpose. This, at last, convinced the Indian, and he admitted Hui-k'o as his first disciple. Training began in earnest and Hui-k'o eventually emerged as the legitimate heir to his master; he became the second patriarch of Ch'an and the first Chinese to be in the line of transmission. This is the central part of the legend: it maintains and underscores the belief of Chinese Buddhists that the transfer of the Zen understanding of the Buddhist dharma was successfully and completely conveyed across the many miles that separate India and China. Even more important, it shows their conviction that the finest tradition of Indian Buddhism—including even the asceti-

Hui-K'o showing severed arm to
Bodhidharma, by Sesshū

cism needed to gain it—was fully absorbed by the Chinese so that it became a new element in Chinese culture.

Bodhidharma is usually known to the Chinese as Ta-mo, to the Koreans as Dalma, and to the Japanese as Daruma. He figures in the popular imagination as a larger than life hero. For instance, according to the Chinese, one of his many gifts to them was a form of boxing that he taught the monks of Shao-lin temple, geographically close to the cave where he supposedly spent his years of meditation. Tradition has it that later, when he had emerged from the cave and was serving as abbot at Shao-lin temple, he became concerned about the poor physical condition of the monks there, noting that they were unhealthy, underexercised, and even emaciated. To build up the condition of their bodies, and thereby facilitate their practice of the Middle Path, he taught them a kind of "boxing." This style of exercise has persisted into modern times and is known by the name of the temple; Shao-lin temple (Shōrinji in Japanese). The attribution of this to Bodhidharma is probably spurious, but the fact that many generations have held to this notion of a close connection between Ch'an/Zen and this type of athletic exercise points to something important in the cultural history of East Asia, namely, the fact that the concept of meditation there is not considered something that engages the mind alone; quite the contrary, meditation has to involve the body as well. Exercises— often grueling and strenuous ones—and sometimes getting involved with the in-intensity of the so-called "martial" arts are part of this way of grasping the mean-ing of the Middle Path. The development of the Shao-lin temple exercises in China was the precursor for what was to be the close connection in Japan between Zen and the military samurai who had the dominant cultural role in medieval Japan for many centuries.

This was not just an accident of history. In fact, the emphasis upon the physi-cal and bodily side of meditation is consistent with Ch'an/Zen's traditionally nega-tive view of too much stress upon the intellect. It is not that this form of Buddhism is anti-intellectual; it is merely a resurgence in the history of Buddhism of an em-phasis upon the role of the human body in enlightenment. Some forms of tantric Buddhism and also of esoteric Buddhism—as practiced in Japanese Shingon, for instance—also stress the role of the body in enlightenment.

The legend of Bodhidharma's nine years in a cave expresses a feat of will but also one of physical endurance. This helps us to understand, then, why the intro-duction of Ch'an into China of the fifth century C.E. was considered so important. After all, Buddhism had already been present in China for five hundred years and had already undergone quite a remarkable development. But those five hundred years had provided a form of Buddhism most appreciated by the Chinese literati, monks, and laypeople who were devoted to the study of texts and to the writing of new texts. By the time of Bodhidharma, Chinese Buddhism included a tremen-dous library of sacred texts, as well as very reverential attitudes about texts them-selves and how they ought to be treated. Books, which then were really scrolls that were unrolled to reveal line after line of vertically written Chinese characters, were highly respected, and the person who could read them and write his own literary text was a literatus, an essentially "civilized" person. Even Bodhidharma, it should be remembered, is presented initially as a man with impeccible credentials on this score: he is an Indian expert on the *Laṅkāvatāra Sūtra*—that is, he is well estab-lished as a man knowledgeable about books and scholarship. But it is this that makes the legend of his nine years in the cave so striking and significant; they are nine years without books or even enough light to read them. Here, in the final anal-ysis, Bodhidharma was perfecting his own enlightenment without the "crutches" of books or the assumption that enlightenment can come from intellectual resources alone. This activity was later to be encapsulated into an important Ch'an principle and the phrase "direct transmission from mind to mind without reliance upon the scriptures." This has been reinforced by the legend—again not corroborated—that Hui-neng (638–713), regarded by many as the sixth patriarch of Ch'an, was himself illiterate. The facts about him are enshrouded in almost as much mystery as those of Bodhidharma,[45] but the point of the tradition is sufficiently clear: literacy is not a prerequisite for enlightenment in Ch'an.

---

[45] *The Platform Sutra of the Sixth Patriarch*, trans. by Philip B. Yampolsky (New York and London: Columbia University Press, 1967).

A central theme in all of this is that what Buddhists called "mind" is not equivalent to the intellect. That is, enlightenment is not the sole preserve of those who are educated and literate. Even though the Ch'an school of Buddhism itself produced vast numbers of its own written texts, the common assumption here is that the mere mastery of texts and theories is no guarantee of enlightenment. Some would go even farther: too much reliance upon texts and too much pride in one's own expertise may prove to be a great hindrance to the attainment of enlightenment. Essentially, it is not the intellect itself so much as the intellectual's ego—that is, his pride in his intellect and how he assumes it sets him apart from other people —that is the real source of the problem here. After all, if enlightenment involves a "letting go" of attachment to one's own ego and self-importance, then the intellectual who wishes emancipation might do well to cease his dependence upon his or her own notion of possessing superior skills or special access through "words and letters."

The cultural impact of Buddhism upon China must be seen in this light. In many ways it was, at least initially, the Chinese literati who relished Buddhism. Through the translations of the Sanskrit texts into their own language, the Chinese people's library of classical texts seemed somehow to be doubled. The earliest forms of Buddhism in China, since they so stressed the mastery of texts, reinforced the importance and status of people who were skilled with such texts—and for the Chinese such mastery was the key to success in many fields, including positions in the government. From early times the Chinese had keyed appointments and promotions to a system of written examinations. The role of reading and writing in Chinese civilization was of vast importance. Perhaps Ch'an posed a large question concerning some of these assumptions; it reminded people that unlettered country bumpkins could also be possessors of wisdom and that the entry into the deepest enlightenment, what the Ch'an people called "the gateless gate," may often require the physical stamina of an ascetic or an athlete. It was not to be achieved by being merely bookish and intellectual.

Ironically enough, Ch'an and Zen themselves have often appealed to intellectuals, perhaps because they promise a correction or "righting" of unhealthy imbalances in the literati's lives. And, as noted, this Buddhist tradition too produced a large number of its own texts. Moreover, some important Zen masters have been quick to point out that Zen does not give license to anti-intellectualism; a medieval Japanese master Dōgen (1200–1253), for instance, curbed any such notion of Zen.[46] It appears that to maintain the course of the Middle Path has required various kinds of "righting" during the many centuries of its history; too much of a pull in one direction has required rectification, a recognition of the importance of the other side.

---

[46] Hee-Jin Kim, " 'The Reason of Words and Letters': Dōgen and Kōan Language," in William R. LaFleur, ed., *Dōgen Studies* (Honolulu: University of Hawaii Press, 1985).

3

difficult places
along the middle path

THE GENERAL NATURE OF DISSENT IN BUDDHISM

The frequent characterization of Buddhism as a "gentle" form of religion and philosophy should not obscure the difficulties, sometimes quite severe, that have arisen during its long history. We have already noted that fairly early it divided into two quite different traditions, best designated today as the Theravada and the Mahayana. In addition, there have been many other bifurcations along the way, sometimes accomplished with ease and good feeling but at other times with difficulty and rancor.

For the most part, however, Buddhists did not force their position on people unwilling to accept them; nor did they try to expunge the lives of those who could not agree with the common consensus. It is one of the interesting things about Buddhism that there is in it no history of heresy, no great concern to eject certain persons from the Buddhist community because they held views at variance with the majority. This is partially because Śākyamuni had told his followers to remember that the Middle Path is primarily a practical one. He specifically instructed them to avoid certain kinds of questions that, although interesting topics for speculation, are not, he said, related to the central need to solve man's problem of suffering (duḥkha). On this point he addressed one of his disciples as follows:

> The religious life, Mālunkyāputta, does not depend on the dogma that the world is eternal, nor . . . on the dogma that the world is not eternal. Whether the dogma obtain, Mālunkyāputta, that the world is eternal, or that the world

is not eternal, there still remain birth, old age, death, sorrow, lamentation, misery, grief, and despair, for the extinction of which in the present life I am prescribing.[1]

Śākyamuni reinforced the point with an important analogy to describe the way in which unnecessary and unrelated theoretical problems actually tend to deflect attention from the matter of most pressing concern:

> It is as if, Mālunkyāputta, a man had been wounded by an arrow thickly smeared with poison, and his friends and companions, his relatives and kinfolk, were to procure for him a physician or surgeon; and the sick man were to say, "I will not have this arrow taken out until I have learnt whether the man who wounded me belonged to the warrior caste, or to the Brahmin caste, or to the agricultural caste, or to the menial caste."[2]

The emphasis was to be on pragmatic, effective means for curing man's central problem of suffering.

This clearly had a restraining influence on the Buddhist sangha. Certain kinds of problems, especially those for which there could be lots of speculation but no empirical or definite proof, questions such as whether or not the world is eternal, were considered unprofitable. The imperative need, as the sangha saw things, was for unwavering concentration on the path to nirvana.

Concerning the teaching or dharma, however, there often seemed to be a surprising amount of latitude for a variety of interpretations. This did not, however, imply an intellectual laziness. In fact, the simultaneous development over the centuries of what are called the various "schools" of Buddhism often permitted the representatives of these differing traditions of interpretation to enter into public debate with one another. Often these debates were sponsored by a ruler or some other prominent person and attracted considerable attention, not only from monks directly involved but from the laity as well. Sometimes it was felt necessary to decide a matter being discussed—and the king or ruler was often asked to be the judge in such cases. But also it was deemed proper to let the debated matter remain pending, a matter of continuing discussion within the larger sangha. Debate, in fact, has often within Buddhism been regarded as a sign of internal vitality; the tradition of forensics has been very strong, and the most highly respected Buddhist philosophers have usually been heralded because of the cogency of their arguments, the sharp-witted nature of their analyses, and their ability to level a devastating critique of the position of their opponents.

Some matters of discussion were, in fact, considered sufficiently important to be debated for centuries and extended far beyond the national and cultural

---

[1] From the *Majjhima-Nikāya,* quoted in Henry Clarke Warren, *Buddhism in Translations* (Cambridge, Mass.: Harvard University Press, 1896, and reprinted New York: Atheneum, 1969), p. 121.

[2] Warren, *Buddhism in Translations,* p. 120.

Monks Debating in Tibet

borders of a single people. These became in some sense "international" or trans-cultural debates and were engaged in on a grand scale. Such, for instance, was the debate concerning whether true enlightenment is "gradual" or "sudden"—that is, does it appear in the life of a person through a sequence of steps leading to higher and higher refinements or does it effect an all-at-once, radical, and thorough change in the mind and life of the person involved? This was a topic that called forth the best efforts of Buddhist thinkers of India, China, Korea, Tibet, and Japan for many centuries. On a smaller scale but also important in its own way was the debate in East Asia as to exactly what was meant by the claim that "all sentient beings had Buddha-nature"; the Buddhists of China and Japan, for instance, wanted to know whether this included plant vegetation as well.[3] When today we look back on the history of these debates and appreciate the serious but unhurried manner in which they were carried on, we can understand not only what Buddhists were thinking about during much of their history but also the way they thought about thinking itself. For them these matters were important not so much because the exact "truth"—as a kind of end product defined at the conclusion of debate—was important but because the *process* of debate and discussion was itself important. Debate and discussion sharpened the mind, stimulated the sangha, and communicated either directly or indirectly to the lay populace that the monks were engaged with important matters.

---

[3] William R. LaFleur, "Saigyō and the Buddhist Value of Nature," *History of Religions,* Vol. 13, Nos. 2, 3 (Nov. 1973 and Feb. 1974), 93–128 and 227–248.

It has sometimes been said that "orthopraxis," or establishing the correct form of daily practice, has been more important to Buddhists than orthodoxy as such. Especially for monks and nuns, the rules for daily life were of crucial importance. Infringements of these needed to be brought to the attention of others so that, through confession and expression of the will to keep the rules from that point on, the orthopraxis of the community could be ensured. If the tendency to violate the rules seemed chronic, the offender was returned to lay life but never relegated beyond the pale of the larger Buddhist community. This matter of keeping the rules has been especially important for those within the Theravada tradition, but all Buddhist monks have had to be concerned with the correct interpretation of the *vinaya* or code for monastic behavior. The vinaya is one of the three "baskets" or major categories of the Buddhist scriptures and includes detailed and exacting rules for the daily life of monks and nuns. The problem has been that from earliest times in Buddhism, there has been disagreement over whether more strict or more liberal interpretations of those rules is correct. According to an important sutra, *The Book of the Great Decease [Passing]*, before he expired the Buddha gave his disciple monks the option of dispensing with certain minor precepts if they so wished. He did not, however, specify *which* ones were minor. Thus when the matter came up for discussion at the first council at Rājagrha, it was decided that, in the absence of clearer guidelines, it was best to maintain that all the precepts should continue to be considered binding.

Although in this sense the "strict" interpretation had been officially adopted, there has always been a suspicion among some that the sangha may have been trying to be more conservative than Śākyamuni really wished it to be; they have argued for more latitude on the Middle Path. This argument for latitude has probably been pushed farthest by some, but not all, Mahayanists. The area of sexual ethics, for instance, is a very good indicator, in part because it occupies such a large place in the codes for monks and nuns. Whereas Theravada monks and most Chinese monks and nuns have traditionally been quite strictly celibate, many Tibetan monks with a tantric aspect in their Buddhist tradition have quite freely had sexual relationships with women. Likewise, in Japan for centuries there were infringements of the strict sexual code for monks; many monks, in fact, had the equivalent of "common law" wives, often semiclandestinely. Later a highly regarded teacher, Shinran (1173-1262), the founder of the school called "True Pure Land" (*Jōdo shinshū*), openly married while he was still a monk. Gradually most Buddhist schools in Japan have since come to the position that even fully ordained monks are permitted to marry and have children. The diversity of actual practice in this matter is fairly great, so much so that when Buddhists from various cultures and parts of the world meet together with one another there are surprises—sometimes even instances of considerable shock—in view of the various ways in which monks live their lives. On these occasions, for instance, there is a great difference between, on the one hand, the strictly celibate monks of Sri Lanka in their yellow robes maintaining a psychological and physical distance between themselves and women and, on the other, the black-robed monks of Japan who sometimes have appeared at "ecumenical" meetings accompanied by their wives.

These things are important. But to understand more exactly what is the contour of a specific religious and philosophical tradition, it is sometimes better to explore some of the things its adherents might prefer to keep at a fairly low level of visibility and also some of the places where that tradition has run into conflict with other traditions, even when it is trying to live in harmony with others in a single and common culture. As a case of the first of these, namely, something concerning which Buddhists have often been ambiguous rather than forthright, we look here at the question of the status of women in Buddhism. And as a case of the second, namely, a friction point between Buddhists and persons of a different perspective, we will study a case of Buddhism's interaction with Confucianism in China. The first is, in some sense, an "internal" problem and the latter one of "external" relations, but both can be very instructive concerning the history of Buddhism itself.

WOMEN AND THE DHARMA

Sometimes it requires certain developments in the recent history of one's own culture to see afresh those in other times or other places. Certainly the development in our own century of sensitivity to ways in which women are portrayed in the past's literature and historical writing assists us to see the whole of that past in a new light. The same is true in religion. In Buddhism, as in most of the classical religions of the world, traditional scholarship and the writing down of the record of the past were almost exclusively male activities since ancient times, and the record reflects this fact. It is quite clear from the texts we have that the status of women, especially the exact nature of their religious role, has been ambivalently treated for many centuries.

That ambivalence was there from early times. In most of the ancient world women were regarded as inherently much less capable of pursuing a religious quest than were men, especially if that quest required physical separation and journeying away from hearth and home. In India the ancient law books had reinforced the notion of women as spiritually inferior to men.[4] In the Indian religious system, women were considered polluted by menstruation and by the expectation that, not being so deeply versed in sacred Hindu scriptures and not being recipients of the protective "power" that comes from holy words and holy books, they were more susceptible to easy attack and even to possession by evil spirits.[5] It is well known that in this context early Buddhism tried to dispense with much of the differentiations of the caste system; entry into the sangha was made available to all, as long as

---

[4] David R. Kinsley, *Hinduism: A Cultural Perspective* (Englewood Cliffs, N.J.: Prentice-Hall, 1982), p. 54.

[5] Kinsley, *Hinduism,* p. 138.

it was physically possible for a person to leave the householding life. But although the break with the idea of religious castes was clear in Buddhism, the granting of a full religious equality to women was not. Archaic notions about women persisted— especially the idea that women will have unusual difficulty in applying themselves with any real rigor and strictness to a monastic life. In a word, women were considered spiritually weaker and more amenable to temptations—especially sexual ones—that might arise. They could not, it was assumed, be expected to stick very closely to the rule of celibacy required within the sangha. The net result was that the early Buddhists took an important step in the direction of recognizing the possibilities of women to practice the Path—a recognition implied in granting them their own order within the sangha—but at the same time made this a qualified and carefully hedged step. All the older presuppositions of Indian culture could not be so easily discarded.

This is detectable in the very conditions under which women were permitted to establish an order of Buddhist nuns. The early code of rules presents Śākyamuni as initially resisting the whole idea of having an order of the sangha for women, although some scholars hold that this whole episode may have been a later invention by male monks and inserted into the text. In this account it is the aunt of Śākyamuni, a woman named Mahāprājapatī, who makes the request, and she makes it not just for herself but for others as well. Then comes the Buddha's response:

> To go forth from home under the rule of the Dharma as announced by me is not suitable for women. There should be no ordination or nunhood. And why? If women go forth from the household life, then the rule of the Dharma will not be maintained over a long period. It is just as if there were a family with many women and a few men. It is subject to easy attack and spoilation.[6]

In spite of this great reluctance, however, the Buddha acceded to his aunt's request and permitted an order of nuns. He did not, however, retract the prediction that this in itself would shorten the period during which the dharma would flourish in the world. Moreover, as if to ensure that the number of nuns would remain comparatively small, the Buddha is said to have instituted additional rules and restrictions upon the daily life of nuns—a rigor above and beyond that required of males.

When we look at these rules, it is easy to see that they were devised to guarantee a continuing imbalance between the order of monks and that of women. A nun, for instance, was expected to show deference to a monk even though he might still be young and someone with only slight experience in the sangha. In this it is clear that, although the very act of permitting an order of nuns was a significant event in India's—and humankind's—religious history, the concepts and attitudes of the traditional culture remained strong. Even though the notion of caste as such was not part of Buddhism's teaching, it was difficult to relinquish completely the bases for inequality between the sexes. If we try to explain why even aged nuns had to

---

[6] *Culla-Vagga,* quoted in Warren, *Buddhism in Translations,* pp. 441 ff.

show deference to younger males, it seems quite clear that this was based on the common assumption that the male was born as a male because of good karma in former lives whereas the nun, however holy in this present lifetime, has not yet been able to assemble quite as impressive a record of good karma *over many lifetimes.* This was the cultural assumption in India, and it is one that throughout the centuries the males within the Buddhist sangha—even outside of India—seldom saw fit to question. If it was seriously considered by women, those questionings have been largely lost to history since obviously it was the men who kept the records and wrote the books.

Since its founding, there has always been an order of Buddhist nuns. The earliest Indian texts of Buddhism tell of a surprisingly large number of women who took the requisite vows. In fact, one of the most fascinating documents of early Buddhism is that called the *Therigatha* or Songs of the Women Elders; it not only includes excellent poetry but is rich with detail about the lives of women who became part of the order of nuns. I. B. Horner in her *Women Under Primitive Buddhism* studied these accounts and their implications. She found in them ample evidence that women had come into the order from a great diversity of social positions and backgrounds. The order was not comprised only of widows or women unable to find husbands. Most important, however, many of these women are presented as being fully realized arhats and some also as influential preachers of the Buddhist dharma. She writes:

དགེ་སློང་མ་རེ་ཤ་ལས་ཆོས་སྟོན་པ།

The Nun Shaila teaches the Dharma Geshe Lobsang Tharchin, *King Udrayana and the Wheel of Life.* Howell, NJ; The Mahayana Sutra and Tantra Press, 1984, p. 19.

As the verses testify, were they but given the opportunity, they were as capable as men of peeling off the wrappings of the flesh, of ridding themselves of sensuality and craving, and of treading on the higher path and of gaining the fruits of arhanship [= arhatship].[7]

This tradition of an order of nuns, although seldom very large, passed down through the centuries and through the various cultures that absorbed Buddhism. The Chinese poet Yüan Hung-tao (1568-1610) writes vividly concerning a woman of his time who has just taken the tonsure:

> *On Hearing That a Girl of the Ts'ui Family Has Become a Disciple*
> *of the Buddhist Master Wu-nien—Playfully Offered to the Master*
>
> She has cut off her conch-shell hairdo,
>   thrown away her eyebrow pencil;
> the passions have been quenched by a single cup of tea.
> Her sandalwood clappers now accompany
>   Sanskrit chanting;
> her silk dress has been recut:
>   a makeshift cassock.
> The Master's mind is like quiet water
>   reflecting this moon.
> His body is a cold forest
>   putting forth this blossom.
> How many times can she remember
>   the hand of ordination
>   on her brow?
> Generation after generation,
>   life after life
>   in the family of Buddha![8]

The number of nuns, however, has been much smaller than that of monks throughout the centuries. Sometimes, as in modern Sri Lanka, it has disappeared altogether. In addition, it seems that examples of enlightened women—except in the *Therīgatha* and a few other places—are correspondingly rare in the sutras, art, and literature of Buddhism. Much more common is the idea that the accumulation of good karma and the achievement of a better rebirth constitute the more legitimate and desirable "track" for the spiritual advance of women. It was commonly assumed, in fact, that the women who showed unusual interest in pursuing the Middle Path would do best to accumulate much merit as a layperson, perfect the virtues of the laity,

---

[7] I. B. Horner, *Women under Primitive Buddhism: Laywomen and Almswomen* (New York: E. P. Dutton, 1930), p. 163.

[8] Yüan Hung-tao, *Pilgrim of the Clouds: Poems and Essays from Ming China,* trans. by Jonathan Chaves (New York and Tokyo: Weatherhill, 1978), p. 68.

and then anticipate rebirth as a male, thus making it possible to gain entry into the order of monks in some future life. Thus, although the earliest records of the sangha give instances of women who as women became nuns and perfected their enlightenment, there has been a strong tendency within Buddhist cultures to adopt the view that maleness is virtually a prerequisite for attainment of the highest ideals. The notion that somehow women, because they are thought unable to keep the rigorous disciplines, actually pose an ongoing threat to male monks was not limited to India; it showed up quickly and frequently in other Buddhist cultures as well. Even common proverbs demonstrate it. In Japan the elephant was an exotic animal and one often used as a simile—because of its strength and freedom to roam —for the Buddhist monk; the point of the following proverb, however, concerns women:

> *With one hair of a woman a great elephant can be tethered.*

The implications of this are fairly obvious.

Nevertheless, the question of the spiritual status of women in the Buddhist sangha remained a sore spot. From the evidence we have, it would appear that occasionally there were those who sensed a discrepancy between Buddhism's rejection of caste and its retention of the notion of women as religiously inferior to men. This is why again and again moves, often tentative and qualified, were made in the direction of recognizing the perfect right of women to become enlightened beings. There can be no doubt that women in the past have found, and today still find, in Buddhism a form of religious practice with a great appeal. Therefore, even though the texts were largely written down and in that way controlled by males, the recognition of the viability and importance of women's quest for nirvana could not be suppressed forever. It evidences itself in interesting and important ways, even in the classic texts.

For instance, the following from the Lotus Sutra, a Mahayana text compiled in India between 100 and 200 C.E., was important both in China and Japan, even though most people today would find one aspect of it objectionable. The sounding of a relatively new motif in Buddhism occurs in a narrative concerning the transformation of the Nāga princess, a mermaidlike creature who is portrayed as being extraordinarily beautiful, exceptionally wise, and complete with all of the virtues of a true bodhisattva. Her conversations are held in the presence of Manjuśri, the great Bodhisattva of Wisdom, and Śariputra, one of the principle disciples of Śākyamuni. These two lavishly praise her virtues, and then, as if in response, she offers to give up as a sacrificial donation the precious jewel set on her forehead— often interpreted to be a symbol of her own female sexuality. The Buddha immediately accepted it and the narrative goes on to say that the Nāga princess challenged Manjuśri and Śariputra as follows:

> I offered the precious gem to the Buddha and he accepted it. Was that not very quick?

They replied: "Yes, very quick indeed."

She responded: "Well, then, you will now see me achieve Buddhahood even more quickly."

Then the multitude saw the Nāga Princess in an instant of time turn into a man and have all the distinguishing marks of a Buddha.[9]

In the Mahayana tradition this was an important episode because many women took consolation in it, even though the necessity of being transformed into a male first would certainly sound peculiar and objectionable to many today. The reason for consolation lay in the fact that the sutra suggested that all the other qualifications for Buddha-hood—the perfection of virtues, the difficult self-discipline, and so forth—were attainable by women while being women. Diana Y. Paul writes that the Lotus Sutra:

> is more liberal in its view of women and more positive in its treatment of the paths of salvation open to women. The paths of the good friend and the Bodhisattva are described as accessible to Buddhist women, in sharp contradiction to the traditional attitudes towards women as obstacles to the spiritual welfare of men.[10]

Fairly early in the history of Buddhism in Japan, for instance, this text was welcomed by women as the one that gave them reason to believe in the Buddhist dharma. For an understanding of early Japanese Buddhism, an important text there was the *Nihon Ryōiki,* a work that features women as heroines in 30 out of its 116 stories. Kyoko M. Nakamura has translated this work into English and in her preface notes that this work, "instead of making negative statements about women, maintains the equality of men and women before Dharma."[11]

Certainly some of the most positive and explicit statements made by a male concerning the Buddha-hood of women came from the famous Japanese Buddhist Nichiren (1222–1282). Nichiren's devotion to the Lotus Sutra as the incomparable scripture of Buddhism led him to see it in sharp contrast to all other sutras. Interestingly, since it is the Lotus Sutra that includes the story of the transformation of the Nāga princess into a Buddha, Nichiren pursued the logic of this and concluded that through the Lotus Sutra women could unquestionably become Buddhas. He noted that in other sutras, understood by Nichiren to have come from Śākyamuni's mouth before the point in time when he was ready to give his final and perfect word to mankind, Buddha-hood for women was deemed impossible. But the Lotus

---

[9] *Scripture of the Lotus Blossom of the Fine Dharma,* trans. by Leon Hurvitz (New York: Columbia University Press, 1976), p. 201 (revised slightly).

[10] Diana Y. Paul, *Women in Buddhism: Images of the Feminine in Mahāyāna Tradition* (Berkeley, Calif.: Asian Humanities Press, 1979), p. 113.

[11] Kyoko Motomochi Nakamura, "Introduction" to *Miraculous Stories from the Japanese Buddhist Tradition: The* Nihon Ryōiki *of the Monk Kyōkai* (Cambridge, Mass.: Harvard University Press, 1973), p. 72.

Sutra, that is, the final and perfected word of Śākyamuni according to Nichiren, presents things differently. Nichiren wrote:

> In the Lotus Sutra for the first time the Buddha revealed that women could attain Buddhahood.[12]

One of the most exemplary women in the history of China and probably the most illustrious in the history of Buddhism there was Ling-chao, the daughter of a famous Ch'an practitioner known as Layman P'ang (? -808). Both she and her father are shown in art as wearers of white robes and untonsured, thus indicating their status as laity rather than monastics. In Chinese Buddhism, however, both are highly revered; they stand in the tradition as models of fully enlightened beings, not just virtuously living laypersons. The recorded sayings of Layman P'ang are one of the treasured documents of Chinese Buddhism. According to tradition, P'ang, having given away his house for use as a temple, placed all his remaining earthly treasures in a boat and sank it in a river; from that point on in his life, he and his daughter made and sold simple bamboo implements for their livelihood.[13] P'ang became the disciple of some of the greatest Ch'an masters of China and his daughter Ling-chao was not only his helper but also herself deeply devoted to the practice of Buddhism. If it can be said that the historic and symbolic importance of Layman P'ang lies in the great enlightenment he had even while remaining a layman, that of his daughter is her great enlightenment while being a layperson and while being a woman, that is, without having either to await rebirth as a male or undergo quick transformation into a male form. Her moment of greatness came especially in the enlightened manner that she finessed her own death; it certainly ranks as a classic instance of an exemplary great death on the part of a woman. The *Sayings of Layman P'ang* state:

> When the time came to pass on, the Layman had his daughter prepare hot water, took a bath, donned his robes, sat properly cross-legged on his bed, and having spoken his parting words addressed her: "Watch when the sun reachs due south at noon and report to me." As he had said, she watched and reported, saying, "The sun has just reached due south, but the sun's *yang* brilliance is eclipsed." The Layman exclaimed: "How can that be?!" Then he rose and went to see for himself. Thereupon his daughter crawled upon the bed, sat properly, and passed away. Her father turned, and seeing this exclaimed: "Exquisite! I spoke it earlier, but I'll now have to do it later."

Accordingly the Layman let seven days elapse and died.[14]

Although there are always hazards in interpreting things that are reported in

---

[12] Nichiren, "Hokke Daimokushō," in *Nichiren: Selected Writings,* trans. by Laurel Rasplica Rodd (Honolulu: University of Hawaii Press, 1980), p. 91.

[13] Ruth Fuller Sasaki, "Introduction" to *The Recorded Sayings of Layman P'ang: A Ninth-Century Zen Classic* (New York and Tokyo: Weatherhill, 1971), p. 19.

[14] Sasaki, *Layman P'ang,* pp. 26–27.

books of Ch'an or Zen sayings, certain implications of this episode seem unmistakable. On the one hand, there is a theme of parental respect and filial piety, things very important to the Chinese: the Layman's daughter cares for her parent's needs right up to the point of his death. Yet, unlike the child of classical Confucianism who simply mourns after the parent dies and performs the required rites of memorial, this Buddhist's daughter is herself a practitioner of Buddhism. Her readiness to pass into death and full nirvana without protest, complaint, or struggle is as deeply grounded as her father's. Moreover, it is significant that both she and her father stand in the Ch'an tradition since in the literature of Ch'an and Zen there is very often an element of levity and good-humored competition even in the final hours of great teachers. Therefore, even at the point when her father had assumed a meditation posture to enter into nirvana, his daughter says something that prompts him to get up to check on the status of the sun—the virtual embodiment of *yang* maleness in Chinese thought. In the interim she takes his seat and promptly expires herself. There is certainly a joke in this. But there is also the suggestion that even in his final and finest hour, Layman P'ang's daughter served him—perhaps then not only as daughter but even as teacher.

Most of Buddhism's history with respect to women would, however, be judged by many as itself far less enlightened. Throughout most of the twenty-five hundred years since Śākyamuni's time, the role of women in Buddhism has probably been only relatively higher than it was in the various cultures where the dharma was taught. Certainly it would seem that if they pursue the implications of the "equality in the dharma" that seemed so important in the Buddha's own sermons, the Buddha-hood of women *as women* should seem clear. It has required the sensitivity—especially that of women Buddhists working in the sociocultural context of the West during the twentieth century—to point out the ambivalence within the tradition and to work toward the existence of a Buddhist community that will eventually practice the equality that would seem logically to follow from Buddhism's own most basic principles.

A BONE OF CONTENTION IN THE MIDDLE KINGDOM

The year was 819 and a Confucian scholar named Han Yü was deeply disturbed about the course of recent events in China. Han, a great stylist both in prose and poetry, was on this occasion composing an essay that he intended to send directly to the imperial palace. It was called a "memorial," in this case a document that protested something that had happened and was at the same time offered to the throne as advice. Han Yü's letter, celebrated even today for its superb style, was entitled "A Memorial Concerning the Bone of the Buddha." It summarized Han's case against the Buddhists and stated exactly why he thought Buddhism ought to be expelled from China, the land traditionally called the Middle Kingdom by its inhabitants.

The context is important to understand. At this point in time Buddhism had been in China for approximately eight hundred years. As Chinese interest in this new import from India had grown, the voluminous sutras had been translated into Chinese. Especially during the period of the Six Dynasties, that is, between 222 and 589, these texts had fascinated the well-educated gentleman scholars of China. Many of them thought of themselves as Buddhists even though the great majority of them had no intention of forsaking their comfortable lives as married men with families to become celibate monks. There were other Chinese, however, who took their Buddhism more literally and actually relished the rigorous and austere practices associated with this form of faith. They were quite willing to become celibate even though this went deeply against the grain of an old Confucian principle that held that being married and having children and grandchildren were indispensible conditions for keeping alive the rites of respect for dead ancestors. After all, the Confucians argued, how can you keep the spirits of the dead ancestors happy and content if you have no progeny to take on the responsibility of carrying out the rituals that so please them? Another thing that the more strict Buddhists in China practiced, and something else that irked the Confucianists, was vegetarianism. This too violated the old ways of the Chinese since the Confucianists had always held that the human species, capable of learning to read and write, for instance, was vastly superior to other kinds. While they appreciated animals and plants, they drew a very strict line between what was human and what was not. Consequently, they thought that people ought to have no qualms about eating *anything* not human. During the Six Dynasties period, the Buddhism that had become increasingly strong in China had, therefore, not only some unconventional ways of thinking about things, but these also involved some untraditional patterns of behavior—things that went against the basic contour of much of Chinese culture.

Later during the T'ang dynasty (618-907) Buddhism became even more deeply entrenched in Chinese soil. Vast monastic complexes in the mountains not only served as places for occasional retreats for laymen but also were the homes for communities of monks that sometimes numbered in the thousands. Temples also were found in the cities and were the sites for vast, colorful rituals and festivals on days sacred to the Buddhists; there one could see throngs of Chinese commemorating the anniversary of the enlightenment or of the peaceful death of an Indian, Śākyamuni, who had lived more than a thousand years earlier. Chinese emperors and empresses also were practitioners of Buddhism and in this way lent their immense prestige and gave of their wealth to the Buddhist clergy and institutions. Since the T'ang was also, at least for the most part, a peaceful era, the Great Wall of China, built centuries earlier along the northern and western borders, seemed somehow to be much less necessary than it had once been thought to be—although the borders were still watched. Free trade and the passage of Buddhists to and from India was comparatively easy in this epoch when China's borders seemed more porous than they had ever been before. On the eastern side of China, people came in quite easily from Korea and pilgrims from Japan crossed the sea to what they called "the Great T'ang" to meet Buddhist holy men and study meditation and philosophy in China's temples and monasteries. To these people from Korea and

Japan, the wealth of Buddhist culture in China indicated to them at least that China now rather than India had become the real "holy land" of Buddhism, the place to go to see a vital Buddhist culture.

To devout Buddhists in China, things had never looked better. But to a loyal Confucian such as Han Yü, the necessity of living in the midst of this Buddhist exuberance was a source of ongoing unpleasantness and mental distress. He felt, for instance, that there was something dangerous about the ease with which the government accepted loose borders in this "ecumenical" era of trade and Buddhism. He knew that as recently as 755, a successful rebellion in the northwestern part of the Chinese empire had turned an enormous piece of China into territory beyond the effective control of the central government. But this physical threat to China's existence was, if anything, outstripped in Han Yü's opinion by his fear that Buddhism was intellectually and spiritually undermining everything that traditional Confucianists like himself had always prized. His memorial to the throne made that abundantly, incisively clear.

The immediate occasion for his protest is evident. On the outskirts of the capital at Ch'ang-an at a place called Fa-men Temple, there was a very precious relic, a bone said to be a piece of a finger of Śākyamuni Buddha himself. Every year this precious object of devotion had been carried into the city itself where it became for a while the centerpiece of a large Buddhist festival. All this had been viewed with contempt by Han Yü. But in 819 things had gone even farther. The bone was said to have been carried not only into the capital but into the palace itself; it had, moreover, been welcomed and worshipped by no less than the emperor. For Han Yü this was the breaking point; he could no longer keep quiet. As a result, he took up his pen and lodged his famous complaint at the gates of the palace.

On the surface of things it looks as if Han was merely being old fashioned and reactionary, a man who thought it was disgusting to see Chinese imitating the ways of Indians. At first his essay almost gives the impression of a writer making far too much of picayune matters of dress and speech—as, for instance, in the following from his memorial:

> Now the Buddha was of barbarian origin. His language differed from Chinese speech; his clothes were of a different cut; his mouth did not pronounce the prescribed words of the former Kings.[15]

But it is important to note that there is much more here than a bit of parochialism or attention merely to "externals." Han is convinced that what people do with their bodies is usually a clear sign of what is going on in their minds. He was in many ways echoing Ku Huan (390–453?)[16] who at a much earlier date had ob-

---

[15] Translation by Edwin O. Reischauer in his *Ennin's Travels in T'ang China* (New York: The Ronald Press, 1955), p. 223.

[16] Kenneth K. S. Ch'en, *Buddhism in China: A Historical Survey* (Princeton, N.J.: Princeton University Press, 1964), pp. 136–137.

jected to the Buddhists because they wore loose robes rather than neatly girdled clothing, because they squatted on the floor "like foxes and dogs" rather than giving the proper salutation or bow, and because they cremated the bodies of the dead rather than burying them in double-layered coffins.

It was true. In becoming Buddhists the Chinese *did* begin to dress and treat their bodies in unconventional ways. Monks wore loose robes, seemed to others to be "squatting" on the floor for hours in postures of meditation, and had their bodies burned on a pyre after death. Moreover, Han Yü in his day knew of times during Buddhist festivals when some laymen were so carried away into ecstasy that they, in the words of his memorial, "burned their hair and seared their fingers in fire, threw away their clothes, and scattered their money, all day rushing about but at the same time abandoning their work and their homes." He told the emperor that he feared this would lead the whole world to ridicule the Chinese.

Another objection was the vegetarianism of the Buddhists; Han warns his sovereign that it had been because of his strict avoidance of meat that an earlier Buddhist emperor, Wu of the Liang dynasty—the emperor Bodhidharma is said to have talked with before going into his cave—had come to a disastrous end. Han Yü writes of Emperor Wu that he

> . . . thrice abandoned the world and dedicated himself to the service of the Buddha. He refused to use animals in the sacrifices in his own ancestral temple. His single meal a day was limited to fruits and vegetables. In the end he was driven out and died of hunger. His dynasty likewise came to an untimely end.[17]

Again, this today may look to us like an argument over trivia. But it was not so at all to Han Yü, and, in fact, his argument deserves careful attention. As a Confucianist he believed that the human body is a gift that an individual received from a long line of his or her ancestors. It is, therefore, something that ought to be treasured and treated well, because in so doing the present owner of that body respects and honors his or her ancestors for their gift. It is, then, a sacrilege to harm the body or treat it in any way other than is "natural." Buddhists, by contrast, often seemed, at least to Han Yü, totally unconcerned either about ancestors or about what happens to their physical bodies. They twisted the latter into various odd shapes for the purpose of meditation and cut off the hair of the head in order to become monks or nuns. Moreover, at least in Han Yü's own day in China, some Buddhists became so carried away into frenzies of devotion that they actually seared off fingers of the body in flames. And for Han Yü all these acts were deeply symbolic ones, because what people do with their bodies tells us a great deal about what is going on in their minds.

A person's diet too is comprised not only of foods but also of symbols. Traditional Confucianists, as mentioned, so emphasized the distinctiveness of what is

---

[17] Reischauer, trans., *Ennin's Travels*, p. 222.

human that they consciously made a point of having no reservations about eating anything else. The line between man and all else was in this way reinforced by behavior at the dinner table; a matter of basic philosophy was at stake there. But the Buddhists were quite different. While they hold that mankind was certainly of a higher order than the "beasts"—because, after all, it required many lives and rebirths before one could rise to be born in the same species as that in which Śākyamuni himself had lived and become the Buddha—Buddhists also spoke about the *continuities* within what they liked to call the realm of "all sentient beings." This concern and compassion for animals led Buddhists in China and elsewhere to practice rituals whereby on certain stated occasions they released captured fish back into the rivers and let caged birds have freedom to return to the air. They also believed in transmigration from one life to the next and, therefore, held that even animals might have been human beings—perhaps even our ancestors—in former lives. Therefore, the Buddhists had ample and philosophical reasons for their vegetarianism even as a Confucian such as Han Yü had intellectual reasons for being zoophagous, an eater of meat. Whole structures of meaning and cultural value lay behind the choices in these matters.

Thus, as Han Yü saw things, what was at stake in his day was the whole question of whether China would culturally and intellectually be what it always had been or whether it would rapidly and unalterably be transformed into a kind of civilization with an Indian rather than a Chinese set of values at its base. And the presence in the imperial palace of a relic bone of the Buddha was for him the last straw. It symbolized, as nothing else could, the fact that the very center of the Middle Kingdom was occupied by foreign ways of thought and behavior. Han wrote to the emperor that, if Śākyamuni were alive and the emperor were to have had only one meeting with this Buddha, he would decide to have the Indian marched, under armed guard, back to the border and sent home to India. He continued:

> How much the less . . . fitting that his decayed and rotten bone, his ill-omened and filthy remains, should be allowed to enter in the forbidden precincts of the Palace? Confucius said, 'Respect ghost and spirits, but keep away from them.' . . . Now without reason you have taken up an unclean thing and examined it in person when no exorcist had gone before, when neither rushbroom nor peachwood branch had been employed. . . . Your servant is truly alarmed, truly afraid.[18]

So he ended his appeal—on behalf of all of China.

Initially, Han Yü's appeal had no effect. It was rejected outright by the palace officials and possibly never even reached the eyes of the sovereign. The very next day Han was himself banished to a place far to the south at the edge of the empire and far away from the capital he so loved. Sometime later in a poem he expressed the irony he saw in this whole situation, a poem addressed to his nephew:

---

[18] Reischauer, trans., *Ennin's Travels,* pp. 223–224.

> *In the morning a sealed memorial was presented through the nine*
> *layers of Heaven,*
> *By evening, dismissed to Ch'ao chou, an eight-thousand mile road.*
> *I wanted to remove certain vile matters for the sake of perspicacity;*
> *Little did I realize that as a decrepit old man I would pity my*
> *remaining years.*
> *Clouds stretch across the Ch'in range—where is my home?*
> *Snow snuffs Lan Barrier, my horse won't go ahead.*
> *I know that when you come from afar, it must be for this reason—*
> *Showing the kindness to gather my bones from beside those*
> *pestilential rivers.*[19]

The poem poignantly shows Han's plight and demonstrates his magnificent sense of historical and poetic irony. The bones of an Indian now lay in the heart of China's capital, and he, as loyal a Confucian as could be found in the Middle Kingdom, faced the prospect of his own bones lying on the outer region of the empire, in a wild and untamed area. What should be outside had been brought into the inner-most place and what deserved to be inside was consigned to the edge of the empire. It was the total reversal or inversion of all that should be. Han Yü depicted what he took to be a China turned inside out.

But Han's exile turned out to be brief. In 820, the next year, he was excused and called back to the capital where he then lived until his death in 824. It is un-known exactly how much his memorial on the Buddha bone influenced the court and the government, but it is clear that the intellectual climate in China soon began to change. Taoists too had raised objections to the sway that the Buddhists seemed to have held over the mind and practices of China. What we do know is that two decades later there was a strong anti-Buddhist movement in China. There was a decree that demanded that the wealth and property of monks and nuns be turned over to the government. By 844 a large number of temples had been forcibly closed; a multitude of monks and nuns had been defrocked. A Japanese Buddhist traveling in China during those years reported that forty-six hundred monasteries had been destroyed there.[20]

This did not mean that Buddhism died in China. But it meant that it accepted now a much more reduced role in the intellectual, social, political, and cultural life of that empire. In many ways, it forced the Buddhists of China to be more Chinese and less Indian. New ways of being Buddhist had to be explored, for instance, the possibility that a monk could do physical labor in the fields without thereby losing the possibility of gaining enlightenment. (In fact, so important did this new mode of practice become that in China it became a tradition that many monks gained their enlightenment precisely while doing physical work, chopping wood or mend-

---

[19] Stephen Owen, trans., *The Poetry of Meng Chiao and Han Yü* (New Haven, Conn.: Yale University Press, 1975), p. 282.

[20] See Reischauer, trans., *Ennin's Travels*, pp. 217-271.

ing clothes, for instance.) The mode of Buddhism called Ch'an became more recognizably Chinese during the subsequent Sung dynasty (960–1279). Moreover, once it was no longer so easy or so important for Buddhists in China to become monks or nuns, a new emphasis upon the Buddhism of laity evidenced itself. Especially for people who, due to their life circumstances or the restrictions of the sangha, could not become monks or nuns but at the same time had no desire to be reborn again and again in order to reach nirvana in some far-off future, a much more appealing Buddhism was that which held that at death the pious practitioner could be immediately transported into the Pure Land.

Many people in China continued to be attracted to the teachings of Śākyamuni on some level. During the Yüan dynasty (1280–1368) the prestige of Tibetan forms of Buddhism and Tibetan monks was very high among many Chinese. But for the most part, the Chinese people came to think of Buddhism as an addition to Chinese culture that did not—and ought not—displace the earlier forms of Confucianism and Taoism there. Buddhism never again gained quite the same hegemony over the mind of the Chinese that it had had during the T'ang dynasty. But neither was it ever expunged from the Middle Kingdom. Along with Confucianism and with Taoism, it remains a part of what the Chinese have liked to call the *san-chiao* or the Three Teachings.

The Three Teachings of Sages, Confucius, Sakyamuni, Lao Tzu, attributed to Josetsu

twenty-five hundred years of poetry

From a very early point in the history of Buddhism, there was something in its dharma that quite naturally expressed itself in lyrical forms. Perhaps this was, at least in part, because poetry and song had always been such an important element in the culture of India, the place where Buddhism came into being. After all, traditional Indian civilization was one that treasured myth, song, and poetry; by contrast, it paid scant attention to history. It is not surprising, then, that the expression of the Buddhist dharma took the form not only of discourses or sermons by Śākyamuni but also in poetic renditions of his sayings and in verses composed by members of the earliest sangha. This was the initial inspiration for a rich tradition of Buddhist poetry, one found in the language of every culture where Buddhism later took root. Although the arts of Buddhism are certainly not to be limited to those of poetry, there may be justification here—in a written text—in focusing upon this mode of Buddhist expression. (Illustrations in this text and, of course, the many excellent collections of Buddhist art can, we assume, tell their own story about the graphic and plastic arts of this tradition.)

Among those early Buddhists who gave up their livelihoods in the midst of society and entered into hermitages in the forests or mountains, there was a strong tendency to celebrate their new style of life as well as their new perspective on life in verse and song, a genre usually called the *gāthā*. Some of the most beautiful of these are in two early anthologies in Pali, the *Theragāthā* or Lyrics of the Monks and the *Therīgāthā* or Lyrics of the Nuns. The imagery of these early poems is powerful.

Just as rain penetrates a badly-thatched house,
So desire penetrates an undeveloped mind;
Just as rain does not penetrate a well-thatched house,
So desire does not penetrate a well-developed mind.[1]

The hermitage of the monk, often as a place of peace away from the maddening world, is celebrated as follows:

The sky rains melodiously;
My small hut is roofed, pleasant, draught-free,
And my mind is well-concentrated.
So rain, sky, if you wish.[2]

But the monk's hut, especially if it were to collapse easily due to the ravages of time or weather, could also stand as a symbol of impermanence (*anītya*) and the shortness of each life we live in the chain of transmigration. The Buddhist teaching is expressed in the implication that new huts are like new lives. New residences are the same as rebirths: real liberation does not come merely by acquiring them:

This is your new hut;
You desire another, new, hut.
Discard the hope of a hut;
A new hut will be painful again, monk.[3]

Not unexpectedly, the Buddhist recluse's decision to leave society often opened his or her eyes with a new appreciation of the natural world, a theme that was to be carried along with Buddhism as it made its way across Asia. An Indian monk struck this note very decisively:

With clear water and wide crags,
Haunted by monkeys and deer,
Covered with oozing moss,
These rocks delight me.[4]

The Buddha's, and the aspiring Buddhist's, spiritual strength and trained control of the passions are compared to a great elephant's gentle power and the way it makes its way through the forest:

---

[1] *The Elders' Verses,* trans. by K. R. Norman (London: Pali Text Society, 1969), verses 133–134.

[2] *The Elders' Verses,* verse 51.

[3] *The Elders' Verses,* verse 57.

[4] *The Elders' Verses,* verse 113.

That elephant indeed outshines others
As the Himalayas outshine other mountains . . .
The elephant's two front feet are gentleness and mercy.
The elephant's other feet are mindfulness and attentiveness;
The great elephant has faith as his trunk
and equanimity as his white tusks.
His neck is mindfulness, his head is wisdom,
Investigation (with his trunk) is reflection on the doctrine;
His belly is the fire-place of the doctrine,
His tail is seclusion.
Meditating, delighting in inhaling, well-concentrated inside
He is a concentrated elephant as he goes;
He is a concentrated elephant as he stands still . . .
He eats blameless things; he does not eat blameworthy things;
Having obtained food and covering, avoiding what has been stored up.
Having cut every fetter and bond, large or small,
He goes without longing wherever he goes.[5]

Buddhism's place of origin, of course, was India, and in a semitropical area that twenty-five hundred years ago was thickly forested. But when it moved north and across the Himalayas to the much colder, mountainous climate of Tibet, it entered an area with a topography and climate very different from the place of its origin. Since its reception in Tibet was bound up with the attainment of literacy on the part of the Tibetans, the themes of Buddhism put an indelible stamp on the poetry of what is often called The Land of Snows. Milarepa (1052–1135), also known as the Cotton-clad Saint, was probably the greatest poet in Tibet's history. In addition, he lived a life the story of which the Tibetans love to retell.[6] That narrative is of a young man who takes revenge on his exploitive stepfather-uncle by learning the arts of black magic and destroying the house and sons of his uncle in one magical feat. But regret over this act of retribution turns him soon afterward to the truth of Buddhism, and he locates Marpa the Translator, who will be his incomparable guru in the understanding of the dharma. Marpa puts him through years of excruciating tests and training; these are often compared to the death-defying trials administered to one who would become a shaman—since shamanism was strong in Tibet before the entry of Buddhism and clearly became a part of it even after the dharma arrived from India.[7] After he has become an unusually accomplished Buddhist yogi, Milarepa sees his dead mother in a dream and travels to his ancestral home, only to find what is left of her there, a heap of bones. Sit-

---

[5] *The Elders' Verses,* verses 692–699.

[6] *Tibet's Great Yōgi Milarepa: A Biography from the Tibetan,* ed. by W. Y. Evans-Wentz (London, Oxford, and New York: Oxford University Press, 1928 and 1969).

[7] Mircea Eliade, *Shamanism: Archaic Techniques of Ecstasy* (Princeton, N.J.: Princeton University Press, 1969), pp. 428–441.

ting on these bones, he meditates and further understands the truth of impermanence. Abused again by his uncle and aunt, he realizes that it had been their initial harshness toward himself that had catapulted him into his study of the dharma. Expressing a theme common in Tibetan Buddhism, he notes that his abusers, or "enemies," turned out after all to be his benefactors and teachers, so he expresses his gratitude to them. He then takes up the life of a nearly naked sage living alone in the midst of Tibet's inhospitable mountains and is visited during the rest of his life by people who come from near and far to glimpse him, taunt him, test him, and beg of him some insight and training in the ascetic tradition he follows.

The verses of Milarepa are said to have numbered 100,000, and this may not be an exaggeration. They are, of course, didactic in nature. Once having attained his enlightenment, Milarepa never seems to doubt or falter. His own verses seem to issue from a mind always lucid, one that celebrates all the spiritual treasures of the dharma as incomparably better than the worldly ones of ordinary society. One day, while meditating by a stream that flowed "like a ribbon of silver," he was visited by a wealthy, young nobleman on a gleaming black horse. This man, a "playboy," comes to recognize Milarepa's saintliness and wishes to provide him with a gift; in turn he offers him a horse, boots, a long coat, a short coat, a turban, a piece of jade, his sister as consort, or, at the very least, a pair of trousers to cover the yogi's nakedness. All are refused because the possessionless Milarepa already has all he needs. For instance, his rejection of the gift of a horse is as follows:

> *Listen to me, dear patron!*
> *A horse of Prāna mind have I*
>
> . . .
>
> *Tranquility within is his adornment,*
> *Bodily movement is his rein,*
> *And ever-flowing inspiration is his bridle.*
> *He gallops wildly along the Spine's Central Path.*
> *He is a yogi's horse, this steed of mine.*
> *By riding him, one escapes Samsara's mud,*
> *By following him one reaches the safe land of Bodhi.*
> *My dear patron, I have no need of your black horse.*
> *Go your way, young man, and look for pleasure.*[8]

In the verses of Milarepa, the austere, awesome, and often forbidding mountain scenery of Tibet forms not only a "setting" in the conventional sense but is itself often transformed into the basics of literary and doctrinal imagery. Hence, the verses become unmistakably Buddhist and at the same time unmistakably Tibetan. Sahle Aui, a woman who is a very devoted follower of Buddhism, comes to Mila

---

[8] *The Hundred Thousand Songs of Milarepa,* trans. by Garma C. C. Chang (New York: Harper & Row, 1962), p. 68.

repa for instruction. She herself eventually becomes a solitary, strong meditator in the midst of the mountains; Milarepa's advice to her is:

> *Listen, faithful Sahle Aui, the woman devotee!*
> *If you want to cleanse the rust from the mirror*
> *of your mind,*
> *Look into the depth of the pure sky!*
> *And meditate in quiet mountains*
> *Blessed by accomplished beings! . . .*
>
> *Like a mountain standing firm,*
> *Meditate with steadfastness.*
> *To win the merits of the Buddha,*
> *Discard both pain and pleasure!*
>
> *Like a river flowing on and on,*
> *Meditate without interruption.*
> *To receive the blessing from your Guru,*
> *You should have incessant faith.*
> *Like the firmament, devoid of edge or center,*
> *Meditate on the vastness and infinity.*
> *To understand the innate Truth,*
> *Unite skill and wisdom.*[9]

The fact that Milarepa's verses were written in the national language has made them, as well as the Buddhist dharma they celebrate, part of what Tibetans have traditionally regarded as their primary treasures as a people.

When it was brought into China, Buddhism at an early date was something to which the literate and learned class—China's famed literati—was very strongly attracted. The reasons for that attraction were many and complex. Perhaps part of it was the way in which the Sanskrit texts, especially when translated into Chinese, depicted India, Indian ways of doing things, and Indian ways of thinking as exotic and fascinating to the Chinese. For the educated writers of China, especially of the Six Dynasties period, Buddhist texts were a rich source for the imagination and full of exciting new literary techniques. Often ways of thinking quite foreign to Chinese ways were introduced through these texts and the writings of the Chinese who liked them. But these strange, outlandish Indian ideas were in some sense "smuggled in" through the literary skills of literati who found that dealing with them was, among other things, a new way of being very sophisticated and urbane. As one scholar noted:

> The skillful Buddhist essayist could at once gain entree to literary circles and cast unwelcome ideas in a welcome form by contriving his essay so that it

---

[9] *Songs of Milarepa*, p. 184.

would seem Taoist to the Taoist, Buddhist to those who understood, and aesthetically pleasing to everyone.[10]

This was, perhaps, a Buddhism of the literary salon rather than that of the isolated hermitage, but it was in any case a medium through which Buddhist ideas and images infiltrated the Chinese mind and Chinese culture.

Hsieh Ling-Yün (385-433) was not a monk but a very learned Buddhist layman. His wealth enabled him to build retreats for monks on his own extensive properties, lands that were transformed by his laborers into a garden of the dharma:

> *A waterfall goes flying past the courtyard,*
> *A lofty forest dazzles at the windows.*
> *In this house of meditation we realize that all is void,*
> *In this temple of debate we analyze subtle truths.*[11]

Compared to the lonely and forbidding Tibetan mountains where Milarepa led his austere life, Hsieh Ling-Yün lived and meditated in a South China setting where Buddhists communed with one another and in some sense with natural phenomena that were approachable and beautiful. J. D. Frodsham comments:

> The presence of these monks in the acadic surroundings of [Hsieh Ling-Yün's] estate indicates to what an extent the monastic career had become fused with the Taoist conception—ever dear to the Chinese gentry—of the life of idyllic retirement and the cult of nature. The ideal of the solitary recluse had to some extent given way to the concept of communal retirement—invested now with a new religious significance.[12]

Or, at least, it came to stand side by side with a continuing tradition of the recluse Buddhist. For in China as in India there were persons who lived as true hermits, trying in that way to follow the dharma.

Two of China's most celebrated Buddhist hermits were Han-shan and Shih-te, men about whom we know very little except that they lived during the T'ang dynasty. The two of them are frequently portrayed in art, always together and always laughing uproariously. About them it is aptly said that:

> Han-shan and Shih-te stand as archetypal eccentric Zen poets—men gone beyond. Gone beyond the clerical stuffiness of the Buddhist Church, beyond the formalistic fussiness of the orthodox poetic tradition, beyond the arbi-

---

[10] Richard H. Robinson, *Early Mādhyamika in India and China* (Madison, Wis.: University of Wisconsin Press, 1967), p. 17.

[11] *The Murmuring Stream*, Vol. 1 trans. by J. D. Frodsham (Kuala Lumpur: University of Malaya Press, 1967), p. 44.

[12] *The Murmuring Stream*, p. 45.

trary constraints of social convention. What are they laughing about we do not know; but what they are laughing *at* is us.[13]

Many of the poems attributed to them may, in fact, not be really from their own pens at all. But the poems themselves are gems. Those of Han-shan, often referred to as Cold Mountain, are already fairly well known in the West,[14] but those attributed to Shih-te are equally expressive of Chinese Buddhism in the T'ang period. He cautions his readers that:

> *my poems are poems*
> *though some may call them sermons.*
> *poems and sermons are just alike*
> *they need to be read closely.*
>
> *go slow; open gently*
> *it's easy to miss the point.*
> *take poetry to be your guide and*
> *you might find out a lot of funny things.*[15]

Many of the best poems of these recluse Buddhists come, however, from those times when they simply celebrate their lives as hermits in the midst of the mountains, far away from the press and pressure of civilization.

> *laughable, these wooded springs*
> *miles from the nearest home.*
> *mist drifts up the towering peaks*
> *where Ribbon Falls cascades down the scarp.*
> *monkeys cry out a long song of the Tao*
> *and the roar of tigers keeps men at bay.*
> *the pine wind sighs sharp and mournful*
> *while the birds chatter and gossip.*
> *all along, I skirt the rocky torrents*
> *or take a solitary stroll along the ridge*
> *sit and meditate against a standing stone*
> *sprawl back to look at creepers up the cliff.*
> *in the distance I see moat and walls*
> *can almost hear the city's bustling rattle.*[16]

---

[13] *Echoes Down a Frozen Mountain: Poems in the Cold Mountain Tradition by Shih-te, Feng-kan, Ch'u-shih, and Shih-shu,* trans. by James H. Sanford and Jerome P. Seaton (unpubl. manuscript), p. 3.

[14] *Cold Mountain: 100 Poems by the T'ang Poet Han-shan,* trans. by Burton Watson (New York and London: Columbia University Press, 1970).

[15] *Echoes Down a Frozen Mountain,* p. 83.

[16] *Echoes Down a Frozen Mountain,* p. 150.

Kung Tzu-chen (1792–1841) was a Chinese poet much closer to us in time and in the degree to which he lived his life in worldly society. For some years he lived the life of the scholar-official, and much of his poetry shows his deep concern about the society of his day and the extent of its corruption. Sometimes his poems were pointed and satirical. In reading the following poem, we do not need to know the references of the various allusions to recognize that the poet is expressing his moral disgust with his contemporaries' custom of painfully binding the feet of women as a mark of beauty:

> *The ancient clothes of the Chi and Chiang clans are*
> *no longer worn.*
> *Like the Chao women, ladies nowadays step daintily*
> *in sharp-pointed slippers.*
> *But when a lord seeks a consort worthy of an ancestral*
> *temple,*
> *Should virtue's reputation depend on delicate toes?* [17]

To Kung Tzu-chen such practices of his day were really serious violations of what *true* Confucianism had intended. His concern for the common people and their plight arose from his understanding of Confucianism, but, according to his biographer and translator, this poet's understanding of the Buddhist teaching of compassion also contributed to the attitude shown in poems such as this:

> *A single hawser takes over ten men to tow.*
> *And at least a thousand boats ply this river.*
> *I, too, once consumed the grain of the imperial granary.*
> *Hearing the trackers' "Heave-ho!" at night, my tears pour.* [18]

In a poem-letter written by Kung Tzu-chen to his wife, there is, in addition to Buddhist sentiments, reference to some past quarrel in the fourth line and an indication that his wife was pregnant in the phrase about a moon dropped into her breast:

> *Your letter full of deep concern made me see your virtue.*
> *I wish to end my frivolity and slowly turn to Zen.*
> *Household cares have long eroded your inner brilliance.*
> *Do not let misunderstanding mar your blooming years.*
> *Watching for flowers in heaven, you pray for commonplace*
> *blessings.*
> *The moon dropped into your breast, leave the outcome to chance.*
> *With a golden Sutra and a stick of incense,*

---

[17] Shirleen S. Wong, *Kung Tzu-chen* (Boston: Twayne Publishers, 1975), p. 90.
[18] Wong, *Kung Tzu-chen,* p. 50.

> *I pray in penitence for you and for me, since dharma is*
> *boundless.*[19]

Kung Tzu-chen, aptly called both religious and romantic, expressed in his striking
poetry a Buddhism which, when compared with that of Han-shan and Shih-te, had
"come down from the mountains" and become mixed with the pressures and problems of domestic and urban life.

Saigyō, by Chōsun Collection of Kimiko and John Powers.

The poetry written by Japanese Buddhists has often seemed to pivot around
this same problem: the choice between celebrating the life of the more or less solitary forest recluse or that of the person who, though devoted to Buddhism, has
chosen to follow the Middle Path into the cities and as part of a "secular" vocation
in the midst of society. The choice almost always appears to have been a difficult
one. Perhaps no poet was ever more tortured by it, however, than Saigyō (1118–
1190). He was born into a warrior family that was assigned to protecting imperial
persons in the aristocratic, refined capital city of Heian-kyō, the urban ancestor
of today's Kyoto. He was simultaneously drawn both to Buddhism and to the practice of poetry and through much of his life felt a painful tension between the two.

---

[19] Wong, *Kung Tzu-chen*, p. 53.

He became a monk at age twenty-three and wanted to live as a solitary recluse in the mountains. Much of his poetry depicts with great honesty the ups and downs of his experience in the mountains, including the difficulty he had in forgetting the glittering life of the courtiers in the capital. Soon after having left the house-holder's life, he spent a winter in the mountains. He wrote that he composed the following after having sat for a long time waiting for trickling water, a sign of the coming spring:

> *It was bound to be:*
> *My vow to be unattached*
> *To seasons and such . . .*
> *I, who by a frozen bamboo pipe*
> *Now watch and wait for spring.*[20]

He could also, however, deplore his own and others' spiritual dullness—but even then with words that did striking things with natural imagery.

> *Delicate dewdrops*
> *On a spider's web are the pearls*
> *Strung on necklaces*
> *Worn in the world man spins;*
> *A world quickly vanishing.*[21]

For years he also sensed a conflict between his "passion" for the beauties of the Japanese mountain landscape—especially the cherry blossoms of spring—on the one hand and his Buddhist vocation on the other. Finally, though, he seemed to have settled this matter so that the phenomena of nature were merged with his Buddhist ideals. Mount Yoshino, one of his favorite haunts and the place he preferred for his hermitage, has been celebrated throughout history for the beauty of its cherry blossoms. Saigyō envisioned it as merged in some deep way, probably through profound meditation, with places in India where Śākyamuni had lived and taught.

> *Do the white blossoms*
> *On my mountain take the place of*
> *Snow on the holy Himalayas?*
> *I wish to enter the profound*
> *Inner depths of Mount Yoshino.*[22]

---

[20] *Mirror for the Moon: Poems by Saigyō (1118-1190),* trans by William R. LaFleur (New York: New Directions, 1978), p. 28.

[21] *Mirror for the Moon,* p. 68.

[22] *Mirror for the Moon,* p. 70.

Few poems surpass the following in its ability to conflate ideals of the Buddhist tradition with the Japanese people's national infatuation with the falling cherry blossom. Saigyō made it a poem that simultaneously looked in two directions: backward in time to the epitome of "fullness"—that is, the parinirvāna of Śākya-muni, traditionally dated on the full moon of the second month—and forward in time to his own tranquil death a few years later.

> *Let it be this way:*
> *Under the cherry blossoms,*
> *A spring death,*
> *At that second month's midpoint*
> *When the moon is full.* [23]

This put the cap on his career; he died as he predicted he would. Subsequent generations were happy to hail him as both an unsurpassed celebrant of nature's beauties and an accomplished Buddhist saint.

A much later Japanese poet was Issa (1763–1827), a writer of the well-known haiku form and a devout practitioner of Pure Land Buddhism. The extremely brief, seventeen-syllable haiku—both in form and content—has often been closely linked to the development of Japanese Buddhism. Haiku's capacity to refresh our ways of seeing things in our mundane world is in its own way a catalyst for "right seeing"—the first point of the Eightfold Path—and deepened compassion. Especially for an adherent of Pure Land Buddhism such as Issa, this motif of compassion, likened to that of Amitābha Buddha, was very important. Issa was one of Japan's best poets. His prose-verse book, *Oraga Haru,* [24] is reconstructed out of his own experiences and reflects not only his many sufferings but also his sense of compassion for fragile and delicate forms of life, especially young children, small animals, and insects. But combined with that sense of compassion was also one that saw other species as involved with man in movement along the Buddhist path. He seems to have been especially fond of frogs, envisioning them as seated so as to do meditation in that position. In fact "Meditation" is the title of the following:

> *giant frog and I*
> *sit staring face-to-face*
> *in silence* [25]

Likewise a serpent's capacity to slough off an entire sequence of skins reminded Issa of Buddhist transmigration through multiple lifetimes until nirvana is reached:

---

[23] *Mirror for the Moon,* p. 7.

[24] *The Year of My Life: A Translation of Issa's Oraga Haru,* trans. by the author.

[25] *Oraga Hara,* trans. by the author.

> *holy temple:*
> *here even a snake shed*
> *its earthly skin*[26]

There was also a horse that surpassed its human master in the capacity for sixth-sense "sight" in the midst of darkness, thus literally acting as its master's savior:

> *bridge shrouded with*
> *night and fog: my horse stops*
> *just before a hole*[27]

Then too there was the fly who prays for mercy to the Buddha-hood in man:

> *spare me! spare me!*
> *pleads the fly, rubbing his hands*
> *before you in prayer*[28]

But Issa's best known poem, reverent even as it shows his agony in face of a personal experience of impermanence, is one in which he responds to the untimely death of his daughter, an only child:

> *the world of dew is*
> *such a world of dew—*
> *and yet . . . and yet . . .*[29]

Issa longs for the Pure Land but is also a poet showing passionate love for the impure, all too impermanent land of the here and now. As such he is rightly representative of a theme strongly present in Japanese Buddhism.

Among poets of the modern West who identify themselves as persons pursuing the Buddhist Middle Path probably none surpasses the American Gary Snyder, born in 1930. Snyder has an uncommon ability to combine the classical Mahayana vision of life, a trained naturalist's knowledge of the details and processes of this planet, and a deep respect for the heritage of native Americans; in fact, he sees in the spiritual life of American Indians striking similarities to those of Zen—which he himself studied in Japan and practices in America as well. The following poems are from his *Turtle Island,* the Pulitzer Prize-winner for poetry in 1975.

---

[26] *Oraga Hara* by the author.

[27] *Oraga Hara* by the author.

[28] *Oraga Hara* by the author.

[29] *Oraga Hara* by the author.

"ONE SHOULD NOT TALK TO A SKILLED HUNTER
ABOUT WHAT IS FORBIDDEN BY THE BUDDHA"
         —Hsiang-yen

A gray fox, female, nine pounds three ounces.
39 5/8" long with tail.
Peeling skin back (Kai
reminded us to chant the Shingyo *first)*
cold pelt. crinkle; and musky smell
mixed with dead-body odor starting.

Stomach content: a whole ground squirrel well chewed
plus one lizard foot
and somewhere from inside the ground squirrel
a bit of aluminum foil.

The secret.
and secret hidden deep in that.[30]

The "Shingyo," which Snyder's son reminds them all to chant, is often used in Buddhist rituals for the dead; it is the Heart Sutra, short and very familiar to Mahayanists, often known, as we say in English, "by heart." (A translation of the Heart Sutra can be found on pages 82–83.)

    The simile of the following poem centers on a fruit that would probably be strange and exotic to most Asian Buddhists, but one that is well known to many North Americans:

AVOCADO

The Dharma is like an Avocado!
Some parts so ripe you can't believe it.
But it's good.
And other parts hard and green
Without much flavor,
Pleasing those who like their eggs well-cooked.

And the skin is thin,
The great big round seed
In the middle,
Is your own Original Nature—
Pure and smooth,
Almost nobody ever splits it open
Or tries to see

---

[30] Gary Snyder, *Turtle Island* (New York: New Directions, 1974), p. 66.

If it will grow.

Hard and slippery,
It looks like
You should plant it—but then
It shoots out thru the
                        fingers—
gets away.[31]

In the Buddhist poetry of China references to the "red dust" usually meant this world of samsara. The final line of the following, a poem set firmly in the American forests of the northwest, probably expresses the Mahayana Wisdom literature position that there is no nirvana apart from samsara.

WHY LOG TRUCK DRIVERS RISE
EARLIER THAN STUDENTS OF ZEN

In the high seat, before-dawn dark,
Polished hubs gleam
And the shiny diesel stack
Warms and flutters
Up the Tyler Road grade
To the logging on Poorman creek.
Thirty miles of dust.

There is no other life.[32]

[31] Snyder, *Turtle Island*, p. 61.
[32] Snyder, *Turtle Island*, p. 63.

5

the dharma:
doctrine and philosophy

Throughout the Buddhist world those who decide to enter into the Buddhist community, whether as a monk or as a layperson, do so by making a simple statement. The visitor to a temple might overhear it being said either in one of the classical languages of Buddhism, such as Pali in Theravada countries, or in the colloquial language of the country involved. It is usually repeated three times. In whatever language, however, it consists of the following:

> *I take refuge in the Buddha;*
> *I take refuge in the dharma;*
> *I take refuge in the sangha.*

In Buddhism this is tantamount to the most basic confession of faith. The Buddha, dharma, and sangha are often referred to as the Three Treasures; when taken together they comprehend every important area of Buddhist ideals, teaching, and communal life.

These have already been discussed in foregoing sections, but the purpose of Chapters 5 through 7, the second part of this book, is both to go into matters in greater depth and to explore how various elements interconnect within Buddhism. The way in which the Three Treasures give articulation to Buddhism corresponds quite nicely to what many find as a useful way of dividing the study of religion into three basic parts: belief, worship, and sociology, in other words, a religion's theoretical expressions, its practical expressions, and its communal expressions.[1]

---

[1] This is the structure suggested in Joachim Wach, *The Comparative Study of Religions,* ed. by Joseph M. Kitagawa (New York and London: Columbia University Press, 1958).

That is to say, "taking refuge in the Buddha" could be said to express a Buddhist's own ideals or highest aspiration in life or, in this case, in the series of lives lived. That aspiration will also be considered worthy of respect and in some sense even of worship. Second, "Taking refuge in the dharma" corresponds to the content of Buddhist belief and Buddhist philosophy; it is the intellectual component of Buddhism, although many Buddhists will wish to insist that its content is richer and deeper than those things we usually discover by our intellect alone. Third, "Taking refuge in the sangha" is a way in which the individual recognizes and declares his or her desire to be part of a larger social unit, the equivalent in Buddhism of what in Christianity is called the "church." Within Buddhism, however, there will be a variety of ways of defining this community; sometimes it will be narrow and at others so broad as to include all sentient creatures in the universe.

By analyzing these three elements in more detail, something of the particularity as well as the internal diversity within Buddhism can be explored. The only liberty taken here is that of slightly changing the traditional order so that we can begin with the theoretic component (dharma), move from there to the practical expression of ideals (Buddha) and finally to a discussion of Buddhism's expression in community (sangha).

Buddhists generally refer to the content of their religious philosophy as the *dharma,* but this word, unfortunately, has a wide variety of definitions and is difficult to pin down exactly.[2] Fundamentally, it refers to the most basic law of the universe—a law, of course, that applies not only to natural objects but also to human behavior. It includes both what humans do and the kinds of things that happen to them as a result. Therefore, according to Buddhists, to be ignorant of the dharma is to put oneself in jeopardy since this law takes effect even when we as individuals do not know about it or do not especially care about it. That is why, to Buddhists, learning about the dharma gives one an inestimable benefit and why they refer to such knowledge as the most precious thing in the world. Such knowledge can make our behavior more rational and moral but also, in the long run at least, brings us happiness rather than woe.

But the word "dharma" is a word used in almost all religions and philosophies that had their origin in India; as such it is not specifically Buddhist. Therefore, to get more exact about the nature of what *Buddhists* mean by this word, we have to discuss another term they use, namely, their reference to Buddhism itself as the Middle Path. This, a term used throughout the Buddhist world and one that many find attractive, is also one that can be very vague. So the question becomes: What exactly is the Middle Path?

This question, "What exactly is the Middle Path?" is one to which I myself was seeking an answer some years ago while in northern India. I addressed precisely this question to a learned Tibetan monk there. He was a man who, although raised

---

[2]Edward Conze, "Dharma as Spiritual, Social, and Cosmic Force," in Paul G. Kuntz, ed., *The Concept of Order* (Seattle, Wash., and London: University of Washington Press, 1968), pp. 239-252.

and educated in Tibet, had traveled also in the West and knew our ways. But now he was living and teaching in India. He listened to my question and immediately responded: "I would like to ask *you* a question. What is the similarity between a beggar and a gourmet?"

Expecting a direct answer rather than a question thrown now in my direction, I was caught offguard. Moreover, his question really puzzled me and my mind stumbled around groping for an answer. I could think only of the *differences* between the two: the beggar will tend to be hungry and gaunt whereas the gourmet will be well fed and possibly even overweight. To me in my very ordinary way of looking at people and things, it seemed that the beggar and the gourmet were on opposite poles in our socioeconomic world; one lived on the bottom of society and the other often somewhere near the top. I could not imagine what they had in common. In the end I was stumped and had to admit that fact. Then the monk smiled and said: "The similarity between the beggar and the gourmet is that each of them spends an unusual amount of time thinking about his next meal. The beggar does it because he has no choice; the gourmet because he has made food into a central thing in his life. But both of them spend a great deal of time each and every day contemplating food—the food they do not have in their mouths at the time. The life of each, therefore, is in some sense being *consumed* by hunger."

What he meant by this, as I was soon to find out by the monk's further comments, is that *duḥkha* or suffering characterizes, as Śākyamuni taught, all sentient life. It is obviously and strikingly present in the man whose gnawing stomach forces him to move along the street searching out scraps of food in the various garbage pails he finds along the way; but it is also present in the man who daily moves along the boulevard going from restaurant to restaurant seeking always to find a dish or delicacy more exquisite than the one he has just consumed. His pain is, to be sure, more a pain of the mind—a certain vacuity in his life—but it is real pain nonetheless. Even his pleasure in eating is immediately linked up with his own kind of suffering and sense of need—at least the need to be recognized and praised by others as a gourmet.

In Buddhist teaching this hunger is usually called *tṛṣṇā*—literally thirst or craving. There is no part of our existence that is untouched by it. A portion of the famous "Fire Sermon" of the Buddha, a text T. S. Eliot once called Buddhism's "Sermon on the Mount," states it very vividly:

All things, O priests, are on fire . . . . The eye is on fire; forms are on fire; eye-consciousness is on fire. Whatever sensation, pleasant or unpleasant or indifferent, originates in dependence upon impressions received by the eye that is on fire. The ear too is on fire. The mind is on fire; ideas are on fire. . . .[3]

---

[3] From *Mahā Vagga*, in Henry Clark Warren, *Buddhism in Translations* (Cambridge, Mass.: Harvard University Press, 1896, and reprinted New York: Atheneum, 1969), p. 352.

And so on. The depiction here of the *extent* of our cravings is unrelenting; the cravings of the mind can be as painful as those of the flesh. Whether we prefer to call it a consuming fire, an ongoing thirst, or a hunger that afflicts both the beggar and the gourmet, it often shows even on the faces of human beings. At least the Tibetan monk in northern India had seen it; he had detected it, he said, in the faces of many young Americans and Europeans, often from wealthy homes, who had exhausted themselves chasing the immediate gratifications of food, sex, popularity, and drugs. Some had literally chased these pleasures to their end. And this, according to what we have seen of the Buddhist tradition, is what Śākyamuni himself is said to have done in his early life; the riches of a prince's life, gourmet foods, and an abundance of women had all been his until he decided to pursue liberation instead.

Then, the tradition says, Śākyamuni went to the opposite extreme—that of extreme asceticism. The first years after he left his family and palace were years spent with holy men who practiced a yoga that was not the body-toning yoga known in modern America but a yoga that was really a self-mortification. Buddhist art representing that period in Śākyamuni's life has him as little more than a sack of skin and bones. The assumption in this kind of prolonged exercise was that the "spirit" will transcend the body and be liberated. As experienced by Śākyamuni, however, this leads really to a new group of desires—the desire, for instance, of having other people look and take notice of what a wonderful and exemplary holy man you have become. The practice of asceticism itself can, as many have discovered, be itself an ego flatterer; the ascetic prides himself or herself on it as something that gives a kind of prestige above that of other men and maybe even a spiritual power over them.

The result is that Śākyamuni discovered and articulated what he called the Middle Path. It is articulated in the eight points of "getting things right" in the way Śākyamuni came to see their rightness. It is a way that finds liberation neither in the pursuit of pleasure nor in the pursuit of ascetic self-deprivation. It finds the way through and beyond attachment to either of these two extremes. For many Buddhists, this teaching concerning a Middle Path is taken as a given and already proven fact. They accept it as true—through their reading of Buddhist writings, through listening to teachers, or even simply by living in the midst of an Asian culture heavily influenced by Buddhism. For them the wisdom of the Middle Path has already been fully tested and proven. They accept it as taught and then lead their own lives trying to avoid both hedonistic and ascetic imbalance, trying to keep their expectations about things, including themselves, realistic, modest, and free of self-delusion.

For others, however, the correctness of the Middle Path is not something merely to be accepted but something to be *discovered*—in the sense that they may even feel compelled to recapitulate the bold experiment of Śākyamuni himself. For them, the following pertains: if the Middle Path is a way that avoids extremes, it can be located only *after* walking the way of the extremes and finding them useless by one's own experience. For this group of people, which some scholars call the "religious virtuosi," both the hardships of asceticism and a deep draught from the cup of sensual pleasures are prerequisites to real enlightenment. The reasonableness of the Middle Path is for them to be discovered, not merely accepted on authority.

Classical Buddhist doctrine goes on to say that among all the things we crave, perhaps the most important is the perpetuation and permanence of something each of us calls his or her own "self."[4] Each cherishes this above all, wanting to believe that some part of us, perhaps a soul or some other kind of invisible and interior stuff, will endure even after our body dies and begins to decay. It is probably our attachment to a notion of our own individual, independent, and substantial self, something the Indians called the *ātman,* that is our deepest, most pernicious attachment. According to Buddhism, it is this notion, a false one at bottom, that leads to the egotism, self-centeredness, and rapacious behavior that makes life on our planet so hazardous and difficult so much of the time. Progressively magnified, it becomes the egotism of families, of groups, of races, of whole societies, and of half a world against the other half.

So the Buddha taught that, if the truth be known, there is no ātman, only fictions in our minds that try to invent one. In his most profound meditations under the tree of enlightenment he analyzed all the elements that constitute human nature and found nothing real that proves the existence of an enduring soul or self. This teaching, a central one in Buddhism, is called the doctrine of no ātman (*anātman*). In itself it constitutes the rejection of a central tenet of most Indian religious philosophy and is a distinguishing feature of Buddhism. It is, however, a teaching that goes not only against the grain of most Indian thought; it probably goes against the human grain in general.

Most people, especially Westerners, often react with considerable annoyance, sometimes even with disgust, when they hear that Buddhism teaches that there is nothing substantial and permanent to the thing we usually refer to as our individual "selves." It strikes them as a teaching that must, then, be a negative and pessimistic one. Looking for an analogy, they tend to envision Buddhism as a teaching according to which what we hold most precious, our individual identities, are swallowed up into some cosmic funnel, merged together into one common mass, and then eventually extinguished, with a mere nothingness as the end result. Perhaps unfortunately, Buddhists often use terms such as "emptiness" and "nothingness" that, unless they are correctly understood, will reinforce that impression of Buddhism as a nihilistic form of philosophy. The problem of getting beyond the surface suggestion of negativity in some of Buddhism's terminology and the need to penetrate to the actual facts of affirmation in what those terms really mean has been a problem that has long plagued and impeded the West's understanding of Buddhism.[5]

The fact is that Buddhists do not envision a cosmic funnel or the amalgama-

---

[4] Walpola Rahula, *What the Buddha Taught* (New York: Grove Press, 1959), pp. 51-66.
[5] Guy Richard Welbon, *The Buddhist Nirvāna and its Western Interpreters* (Chicago and London: University of Chicago Press, 1968).

tion of all individuals into a common lump. Even the more mystical aspects of Buddhism do not hold that the particulars of our experience are unreal—merely the ghostly, insubstantial appearances of something else behind and underneath them that is more real and substantial. Buddhists do not so much deny the reality of the things we experience as they deny their permanence. They insist that all the particulars we know—including the ones that presently respond when our individual names are called—are bound, sooner or later, to succumb to the law of impermanence (anitya); every "thing" in existence is really a changing constellation of other "things" and is, even while we observe it, already undergoing a reconstellation into something else. Buddhists, therefore, say that all these particular things lack independent existence or "self-being." Buddhists recognize that, at least when it is first encountered, this is a difficult and probably even an unpalatable teaching. But they maintain that it need not remain repugnant; if pursued deeply and reckoned with adequately, it can yield a profound sense of reassurance and fundamental cooperation with the laws of the universe. To place oneself in a fully aware condition of harmony with these laws, the dharma, is tantamount to gaining a sense of great peacefulness. It also, so the Mahayanists claim, allows one to reduce friction and to learn how to be in a state of deep "play" in the midst of the universe.

The point is that the term "emptiness" (*śūnyatā*) too can move from being heard and perceived as threatening to a point where it is understood as something affirmative. It first sounds like a deprivation; after all, who likes an empty lunchbox, an empty pocketbook, or an empty life? But then when we realize that it is really the co-dependence and mutual cooperation of all things—and the "play" of all things—that is meant, śūnyatā or emptiness comes to be seen as a fulfillment. Historically it became especially important in the development of the Mahayana.[6] The philosophical groundwork was laid for this already in the thinking of Indian Buddhists, and it has its finest expression in statements of the *Prajñā-pāramitā* or Wisdom literature. Perhaps the best known of these is what is usually called the Heart Sutra; because it is also the shortest, most compact, and most memorable of Buddhist sutras, it can be included here in translation.

The Heart Sutra

Avalokiteśvara, a seeker of Awakening of the world as well as of himself, when he practiced in the profound perfection of ultimate knowing, thoroughly realized that the five components of man's being were all empty of their self-nature, and thus had all the sufferings and worries extinguished. The physical component is none other than emptiness; emptiness is none other than the physical component. The physical component is emptiness; emptiness is the physical component. This is also true of the other four, mental components: sensation, representation, will, and consciousness. All that has its own characteristic or form, is empty of form: no arising, no ceasing, no

[6] Edward Conze, *Buddhist Thought in India: Three Phases of Buddhist Philosophy* (Ann Arbor: University of Michigan Press, 1967), pp. 60 ff.

contamination, no lack of contamination; no increase, no decrease. Therefore, in emptiness is no physical component, no sensation, no representation,
no will, no consciousness, no eye, no ear, no nose, no tongue, no body, no
mind; no shape or color, no sound, no smell, no taste, no touch, no concept;
no visible world nor any consciously perceivable world; no ultimate ignorance, no extinction of ultimate ignorance, nor any aging-dying, nor extinction of aging-dying; no suffering, no cause of suffering, no extinction of
suffering; no practice which leads to the extinction of suffering; no knowing,
no attainment. Because of non-attainment, the seekers of Awakening of the
world as well as of themselves, resting on the perfection of ultimate knowing,
have their mind freed from all hindrances. Because of no hindrances they are
free from all fears, perversions, and delusions. This culminates in their attainment of ultimate calm. All the Awakened ones in the three divisions of time,
past, present, and future, by resting on the perfection of ultimate knowing,
have attained the unsurpassed right Awakening. Therefore, it should be
known that the perfection of ultimate knowing, a great formula, a great formula of knowing, an unsurpassed formula, an unequalled formula, a formula
which calms all sufferings, is truth because it has no falsity. In the perfection
of ultimate knowing is a formula uttered such as: Attained, attained, perfectly attained. Upon being perfectly attained: Oh Awakening, Bliss! Thus
concluded is the Prajñā Heart Sutra.[7]

The Heart Sutra is memorable and even memorizable; in Japan during a brief
period in the 1970s it even became the lyrics for a popular song. Being memorizable, however, does not make the Heart Sutra immediately intelligible. Long commentaries and whole books have been written to explain and make it clear.[8] Here
it is presented primarily to provide a taste of the style and language of one of the
finest Mahayana texts, one that can be quoted in full because of its unusual brevity.
It is like the earliest sutras in that it too takes the form of a diagnosis, sometimes
almost medical in tone, of reality into its various parts. However, on another level it
expresses the freedom and even the playfulness of the bodhisattva—Avalokiteśvara,
the Bodhisattva of Compassion.[9] This bodhisattva, known in China as Kwan-yin
and in Japan as Kannon, is portrayed here as looking on with pleasure and insight
into the structure of reality. This sutra originated, of course, in India—even though
it was probably not *typically* Indian. The icons of Avalokiteśvara were at first male
but over the centuries increasingly took on female characteristics, so that today
we might legitimately say either "he" or "she" when referring to this bodhisattva.
Part of the purpose of the Heart Sutra, however, is not to contemplate a far-off
bodhisattva who is contemplating reality but to become *identified* with him or
her—to become such a bodhisattva oneself.

---

[7] Translation by F. A.S. Society, Kyoto.

[8] For example, Edward Conze, *Buddhist Wisdom Books* (New York: Harper & Row,
1958), pp. 77–107.

[9] C. N. Tay, "Kuan-yin: The Cult of Half Asia," *History of Religions,* Vol. 16, no. 2
(November 1976), pp. 147–177.

One fascinating aspect of this sutra is that Avalokiteśvara contemplates the structure of reality but at the same time does so in a spirit of great, deep play. It might even be said that this sutra puts to music Nāgārjuna's point about nirvana not being separate from samsara. The great bodhisattva contemplates the world not to distance himself or herself from it but to live right in the midst of it with an attitude of spiritual playfulness. As such, this fits in well with a very characteristic type of thinking found in East Asia, where even "mystical thinking" does not so much try to remove the mystic from the world but seek to

> discover a new viewpoint on normal experience that makes the continuing experience of the normal a mystical experience in itself.[10]

Once understood as being at "play" in the midst of the universe, the bodhisattva and even the Buddha could be represented in lovable, cheerful, even humorous forms in China, Korea, and Japan. This easily led to a mixture of these notions with older ideas of the Taoist holy man as a delightful, sometimes crazily delightful, childlike being at play in nature or society.

BUDDHAGHOSA: A CLASSICAL THERAVADA THINKER

Throughout the Buddhist world it is customary for a person to be given a new name when he or she formally becomes a member of the Buddhist community. This, of course, is especially so when someone becomes a monk or nun; then the head is shaved, the robes of monk are donned, and he or she is formally declared to have left the householder's way of life; in some sense the new name suggests the person has begun a new life. At least the new name, referred to as the dharma-name, indicates a deep aspiration and a commitment.

The Buddhist name of an Indian monk who lived at the fourth century and beginning of the fifth century C.E. and spent most of his life as a philosopher of the dharma in Sri Lanka has always seemed especially apt.[11] We have no inkling of what his original name might have been; he has been known for centuries by his dharma-name, Buddhaghosa, the Voice of Enlightenment. As a name, it depicts accurately the clarity and authority with which his writings have articulated the dharma as understood within the Theravada tradition. His is *the* classical exposition—logical, clear, and enduring. His dates are roughly the same as those of St. Augustine of Hippo, probably the greatest doctrinal father of early Christianity; quite rightly, perhaps, Buddhaghosa's role in Buddhism has often been compared to that of Augustine's in the development of Christianity.

Buddhaghosa's writings are a good place to look in order to see the ways in

---

[10] Lee H. Yearley, "Three Ways of Being Religious," *Philosophy East and West,* Vol. 32, no. 4 (October 1982), pp. 440–451.

[11] Bimala Charan Law, *The Life and Work of Buddhaghosa* (Delhi: Nag Publishers, 1976).

which what is called "meditation" in Buddhism often overlaps with what is called philosophy. Although he wrote commentaries on each of the three groups or "baskets" (*Tripitaka*) of classical Buddhist texts, his major work in Pali is called the *Visuddhi-magga* or *Path of Purity*.[12] Its first part deals with virtue or morality and goes into great detail to define and justify the multitude of regulations that were traditionally part of the life of a Buddhist monk or nun. The things said to lead to impurity are many, and they are proscribed not so much because they are inherently evil but because they tend to deflect a monk or a nun away from the goal of nirvana, a goal that, according to Buddhaghosa, can only be achieved through total concentration. Sex, property, preoccupation with food, even the deserved fame of a saintly monk: these things are worthless when compared with the goal of nirvana, and they are to be shunned because they will tend to deflect the adept in his pursuit of that goal. The fact that this section is first in Buddhaghosa's work is due to the fact that the purification of one's way of life would be the initial step taken by anyone aspiring to follow the Middle Path—especially in the Theravada tradition. Without it the later stages would be effort taken in vain.

The second major portion of the *Vissudhi-magga* deals with "concentration"; in it Buddhaghosa describes many activities that we would identify as meditations. These are described and analyzed in considerable detail. Buddhaghosa very matter-of-factly tells the aspiring meditator to choose some object on which to focus and gives ten examples—things such as a circle drawn on clay, a bowl of clean water, a flame seen through a hole, air shaking a treetop, and the like. He then takes the first of these—a circle drawn on clay, called the "earth device"—and gives the procedure for meditating through the use of it. He advises that the person get free of all distractions guarding the gates of the senses. Then he suggests that the person should place the circle about a yard from where he or she is sitting and focus on it with the eyes partially open, repeating at the same time the word for "earth" again and again. Then the eyes are to be opened and shut until a clear "afterimage" on the retina of the eye is retained; this is to be repeated until that afterimage can last for a night and day. After this the adept will know considerable serenity.

But this is only a precursor of what is to come. Buddhaghosa wants his follower to take up what is called Meditations on the Foul—something that concretely refers to the intense observation of decaying corpses. He tells the aspirant to go to one of the cemeteries outlying the city or village, a place where—apparently, at least, in Buddhaghosa's own time—one could find unburied and uncremated corpses lying in their decomposing state. Buddhaghosa is very detailed and anatomical about what exactly a decayed corpse looks like; he refers to it as trickling with juices "like a grease pot." In all of this, of course, he insists that such a corpse is the quintessence and empirical proof of the fact of impermanence, an inescapable aspect of the existence of each of us. He goes into detail because he wants a person

---

[12] Buddhaghosa, *The Path of Purity*, 3 vols., trans. by Pe Maung Tin (London: The Pali Text Society, 1923–31).

to follow the meditation to the point where he has overcome the sense of revulsion and fear.

So he advises as follows: Sit at night in a cemetery where corpses lie uncovered and in obvious decay. Focus on such a putrefying body until you are able to see it, like the circle on clay above, even with the eyes closed. Then, when you can keep the presence of the corpse in the mind's eye even with the eyes closed, begin to return home. Along the way you will come to be terrified by the vision of the dead one and it will become "as though standing up, towering above, and chasing you for dear life." You will have the sense that this corpse chasing you is, in fact, your own. Then, when your hair is standing on end and terror fills your whole being, you will suddenly come to your senses; you will reestablish your mindfulness and tell yourself:

> "But a dead body is not known to get up and chase anyone! . . . If a rock does not move, why should a corpse? This illusion of mine is made by my own imagination. Fear not, Monk!"[13]

Then laughter will arise in you, and you will be able to drive on to the ecstasy of the great enlightenment.

This last point is very important and should not be misunderstood. Buddhaghosa is not merely interested in providing an exercise for people to rid themselves of superstitions about corpses and ghosts or the childish fear that they may in fact be able to move. The laughter he tells us that will come at the end of this meditation is not merely the delight of the person who has finally put away a child's fear of bogeymen, coming to see them as silly and baseless. Buddhaghosa's point is quite different; at the end of this meditation—if it is carried out as it should be—he envisions "the ecstasy of the great enlightenment," something much more profound and rare than merely a sense of having outgrown childish notions and childish fears.

The important thing is that this meditation forces a person to envision his or her own body being the habitation for creatures other than that person's own soul or spirit. In fact, Buddhaghosa stresses that through this painful procedure, a person can realize that his body is, in fact, "owned" by other creatures as well. He will overcome his sense of exclusive proprietorship and even his false sense of self. He will stop lusting after the "what-is-mine idea." The deep ecstasy will arise from the sense of liberation this gives.

Elsewhere he writes about this:

> Already we share our bodies with 80 classes of parasitic animals and in dying our bodies will become the possession of snakes, scorpions, and worms. The body I think of as *mine* is, in fact, a shared one.[14]

---

[13] *The Path of Purity,* vol. 2, pp. 214–215.

[14] *The Path of Purity,* vol. 2, p. 220.

If anything Buddhaghosa's calculation here was an underestimation; modern micro-biologists count at least 100 billion microbes on a man in one day alone. In *Life on Man* Theodor Rosebury writes:

> Thus we are populated. Microbes cling to us where they can, living in their own way. . . . While we stay healthy their aggregates resemble the Coney Island crowd or the rush-hour subway jam only at the end of the alimentary trail, where, indeed, they merely accumulate at the gates, awaiting expulsion.[15]

The point here is that this is not an unnatural condition; it is not, in fact, a condition we could live without. The facts are indisputable; the only difference is that what the microbiologist points out to be a fact of our biological existence is by Buddhaghosa turned into something indicating that we should not get caught in the illusion that there is some permanent "self" that is somehow the unique "owner" of the body in question. That is, the Theravada philosopher, having in some sense used meditation as his own "laboratory," has recognized not only that we are extensively populated but, in fact, ought to push this fact to its philosophical and psychological conclusion. This would be the acceptance of what Buddha had taught were the Three Marks of existence: impermanence, suffering, and no-self. According to Buddhaghosa, the final result, then, of all this extensive confrontation with the real facts of our existence—and the inevitable fact of our death—is control, freedom, and a life that can be lived with mindfulness concerning both life and death. The meditations on death, therefore, instead of being morbid exercises leading to a pessimistic view of things, turn out to affirm not only a realistic view of things but also, according to Buddhaghosa, a liberated one—liberated in the sense that it is free from crippling illusions. Buddhaghosa writes that it arouses "joy and happiness in the meditator."

Before going on with an account of the *Vissudhi-magga,* there may be value in simply noting that this "meditation on the foul" and especially its motivation have frequently been misunderstood and misinterpreted by Westerners. On hearing accounts of monks going to cemeteries to meditate or seeing paintings from Tibet and Inner Asia that depict cemeteries and corpses, nineteenth- and early twentieth-century Westerners jumped to the hasty but wrong conclusion that Buddhism was a morbid, death-obsessed form of religious philosophy. Likewise, when they heard that Japanese schoolchildren traditionally learned their equivalent of the ABC's with a limerick referring to life as cherry-blossoms that quickly fall to the ground and die, these Westerners concluded again that Buddhism even in East Asia was a philosophy of deep pessimism that had historically spread from India throughout most of Asia. The reader of Buddhaghosa's *Path of Purity* can, by contrast, quickly see what was wrong with that kind of judgment: it took things completely out of

---

[15] Theodor Rosebury, *Life on Man* (New York: Viking Press, 1969), p. 48.

their context. It failed to see that in Buddhism the mention of death and decomposition are traditionally taken as the "strong medicine" that is designed to wean us away from fantasies about ourselves as permanent entities in our world. In their own context such meditations as those on the foul—or, for instance, the Tibetan paintings that show similar things—are designed to be part of a much larger process of meditation on reality and liberation from illusion. The texts as well as the people who have performed such meditations interpret them as leading to a new sense of freedom and happiness.

It is impossible here to treat all of Buddhaghosa's rich text. The development of meditations directed to the virtues of social or interpersonal life, however, is also important. One of these, of course, is that of "love" (*maitrī* in Sanskrit or *mettā* in Buddhaghosa's Pali). Here too the way of handling an attitude such as hatred is by way of a personalized analysis. A person must ask him or herself:

> In getting angry with this man, with what art thou angry? Art thou angry with the hairs on the head? Or with the nails . . . urine? Or art thou angry with the earthly element, the watery element . . . ? Or with the aggregate of feeling . . . ? With the element of mind? With mind-cognition? When he analyzes the elements thus, there is no place for anger as there is none for a mustard seed on the point of an awl, or for a painted picture in the sky.[16]

After this exercise it is assumed that the anger will have left. The vacuum is to be filled with something else:

> Thus, with the hatred dispelled, he should direct thoughts of love towards his enemy just as he does towards a dear person, a very dear person, or a neutral person.[17]

This, it is said, "breaks down the doors." If done properly it also, according to Buddhaghosa, leads to a new degree of ecstasy and happiness.

Persons who have read this work closely have noted that it is based on a principle that runs throughout the Buddhist tradition—that is both in the Theravada and Mahayana. It is referred to as a type of meditation that really combines two elements: *samatha-vipassanā* (in Pali) or tranquility and insight.

The first, *samatha,* is really the mind-work that leads to a mystic state, a frame of mind that is clearly different from that of everyday consciousness. Even Buddhist scholars admit that this is basically derived from Indian yoga practices and is not purely Buddhist. It is the second aspect, *vipassanā,* that introduces the specifically Buddhist dimension.[18] It designates the move to acquire insight and understanding; it comprises the final portion of Buddhaghosa's great treatise. On

---

[16] *The Path of Purity,* vol. 2, p. 352.

[17] *The Path of Purity,* vol. 2, p. 353.

[18] Rahula, *What the Buddha Taught,* p. 68.

the one hand, it is the logical rationalization for everything described earlier, and on the other hand, it is the specifically Buddhist insistence that mere trances and enjoyable mental states are not sufficient. Without insight into the nature of things and a new capacity for clear-sighted viewing of the world around one, the first part, according to Buddhaghosa at least, does not give the full liberation that is within the reach of man.

One of the fascinating aspects of modern studies of the Buddhist tradition, especially those by contemporary Japanese scholars, has been the discovery that this emphasis upon both samatha and vipassanā runs throughout the Buddhist tradition. Even though the languages and cultural fashions of East Asia are often so different from those of India and Southeast Asia, there is a remarkable continuity in this. In medieval Chinese treatises on Buddhist philosophy as well as in the writings of Japanese poets concerning meditation and their views of poetry, the connection between samatha as tranquility and vipassanā as insight is very clear. It is interesting and important that precisely that feature where Buddhism, having absorbed much of the pan-Indian practice of yoga, goes off in its own special direction is the one that seems to have made its way through various and thick cultural walls in order to become a common element of the entire Buddhist tradition. It is one that Buddhaghosa depicts with a clarity that quite naturally has made his works into classics for the tradition.

KEIJI NISHITANI: A MODERN MAHAYANA THINKER

Opinions differ, both among Japanese and outside visitors to Japan, concerning the condition of Buddhism there today. Some say it remains surprisingly strong, although so deeply embedded in the culture and the thought habits of the people that it does not always make its presence very obvious. They say you have to look through the fact that the Japanese are now a supermodern nation to the fact that traditional ways, and often very Buddhist ways, are still present and are making an impact on the way people think and behave. Others say that Buddhism in Japan has become primarily something found in temples that are today mostly for tourists and for carrying out funeral services. They insist that Buddhism's low profile there, especially in the vast urban centers where so much of Japan's population now lives, points to the fact that Buddhism there has become moribund for most people. Its beliefs and traditions have experienced a rapidly decreasing relevance in an age of computerized intelligence, robot-operated technologies, and the possibility of living "the good life" through all these things.

Without trying to come to a final answer on that question, it is important to note that in the midst of vast changes in twentieth-century Japan, there has also come into being there something unique, that is, a "school" of philosophy that claims to be based on classical Buddhist thought while at the same time being thoroughly modern. Whether or not Buddhism among the masses in Japan is alive or moribund, there can be little doubt that this development, usually called the Kyoto

School, has been energetic, productive, and creative throughout most of the twentieth century. Its founder was Kitarō Nishida (1870-1945), a name that all educated Japanese know as the undisputed "father" of modern philosophy in Japan. Nishida taught philosophy in Kyoto, the ancient city that was Japan's capital from the eighth century until modern times and a city that still today has worldwide recognition for its many beautiful, old Buddhist temples, its gardens, and the continuing devotion of its inhabitants to Buddhist-influenced cultural practices such as the traditional tea ceremony. Nishida taught at Kyoto University, where he trained many of his best students to become philosophers themselves. Some of them formed a constellation of thinkers that for the most part has been continuously eager to articulate the importance of Buddhist-based kinds of thought in the midst of thoroughly modern contexts.

Perhaps what has made the members of the Kyoto School so effective and interesting, however, has been the fact that they all followed Nishida in first getting a thorough knowledge of Western languages and philosophical thought before trying to articulate what it meant to them to be modern thinkers whose philosophy had a Buddhist basis. They wrote their books first of all for their fellow Japanese, but quite a few of these books have over the years been translated into Western languages as well. Consequently, a gradual awareness of the Kyoto School has been growing in Europe and America too.[19] What has interested outside readers of these philosophers has been precisely the problem of what a Mahayana Buddhist form of thought would look like when expressed in the "language" of twentieth-century Western philosophy.

Among living representatives of the Kyoto School, the most important is Keiji Nishitani, someone who undoubtedly has also been the most important Japanese philosopher of the second half of the twentieth century. Thomas J. J. Altizer, in fact, in 1984 called Nishitani "the most distinguished living Eastern thinker."[20] Born in 1900, Nishitani is clearly a man of this century, aware for instance of the profound impact that science has made on all our lives. Early in his own studies he distinguished himself as a brilliant disciple of Nishida; he taught at Kyoto University for forty years and also held visiting professorships in America and Europe—as well as being a prolific writer. His understanding of philosophy is matched by an interest in traditional Japanese culture. He has written, for instance, perceptively about the poet Bashō. In showing this interest, he demonstrates the influence of another Kyoto School philosopher, Shin'ichi Hisamatsu (1889-1980), the author of an important study of Zen and the arts.[21]

---

[19] *The Buddha Eye: An Anthology of the Kyoto School,* ed. by Frederick Franck (New York: Crossroad, 1982).

[20] Thomas J. J. Altizer in a review of Nishitani's *Religion and Nothingness* in *Journal of the American Academy of Religion,* Vol. 52, no. 1 (March 1984), 198.

[21] Shin'ichi Hisamatsu, *Zen and the Fine Arts,* trans. by Gishin Tokiwa (Tokyo: Kodansha, 1974). Another representative of the Kyoto School is Masao Abe; see his *Zen and Western Thought,* ed. by William R. LaFleur (Honolulu: University of Hawaii Press, 1985).

Nishitani holds that the most important concept in Buddhism is that of *śunyatā* or emptiness, and he maintains that it can be an especially good corrective for a good deal of the lopsided thinking he detects in much of modern Western philosophy. Nishitani prefers to use the word śunyatā rather than emptiness, probably because most people think that "emptiness" refers to some sort of absence, lack, or deprivation and are convinced that it cannot be very good or agreeable. As noted earlier, our everyday language tells us this much: Who, after all, prefers an empty plate or wants to lead an empty life? Therefore, one of the important things to learn about śunyatā is that it is not such a negative term. In fact, Nishitani follows most of the Mahayana thinkers in conceiving of śunyatā as an entree into a new vision of the freshness and *beauty of particulars*. It does not in any way swallow them up or forge them into an undifferentiated mass. A good proof of this lies in the fact that the Mahayana teaching of emptiness led many of those who understood it into the writing of poetry and the painting of pictures that exfoliated with rich details. Śunyatā does not at all lead to the devastation of phenomena, feelings, and mind that we in the West usually associate with the term "emptiness."

Why so? Why is śunyatā so worthy of attention and understanding? Why does Nishitani spend so much effort exploring it in his most important work, one now translated into English as *Religion and Nothingness*? It is because śunyatā in Nishitani's view is expected to do some new and very important work in our minds, the work of dislodging some old but deeply entrenched notions there. One of these is the jettisoning of the notion of a thing's substance or self-identity—a notion we saw being progressively dismantled by early and Theravada thinkers as well. Needless to say, Nishitani has done the same—but in the twentieth century. He has written at a point in time when what have sometimes been called the "acids of modernity" have been dissolving man's traditional belief in deity and also seem to be constantly threatening man with "meaninglessness," giving him the feeling that individual lives and even the whole of the universe have no real purpose. It is this that Nishitani has called the threat of nihility, and he has not at all been surprised to find it in the midst of modern man's world. What Nishitani wants, however, is for us to stop treating the *nihil* (the Latin word for "nothing") as something *out there,* objectified, and held away from ourselves. For him the impermanence of things (anitya) is not separate from their being, like something outside that comes toward us like an *external* threat, but is bound up with their being from the very beginning. He writes:

> It matters not how gigantic the mountain, how robust the man, nor how sturdy the personality. Nihility is a question that touches the essential quality of all things.[22]

Nishitani wants to go further with nothingness. He wants us to allow our-

---

[22] Keiji Nishitani, *Religion and Nothingness,* trans. by Jan Van Bragt (Berkeley and Los Angeles, Calif., and London: University of California Press, 1982), p. 122.

selves to be pushed even further by it so that we realize the "necessity of having nihility go a step further and convert to śunyatā."[23] Nishitani calls this śunyatā the source of all things but quickly goes on to say that "source" here is not like we usually imagine a source to be, that is, some kind of point *behind* the things we see with our eyes and think with our minds. Nishitani insists that we do not have to go *elsewhere* to find the source of things—the way people usually "think of God or the world of Ideas as lying in the beyond."[24] We can learn all we need to know about things and their source from those things themselves. He quotes a haiku poem by the great poet Bashō (1644–1694):

> *Go straight to pine*
> *trees to learn of pine*
> *and to bamboo stalks*
> *to know bamboo.*[25]

Stating that the field of śunyatā is nothing other than the field of great affirmation, Nishitani holds out for a vision of the world in which every phenomenon is permitted to be the center of the universe. This, of course, drastically changes the meaning of "center," but this change is tantamount to a kind of conversion.

And it is not that this is easy. Nishitani insists that what happens is at bottom *deeply religious,* although it does not depend on the existence of God or of gods, and involves a complete turnabout in our way of looking at the world:

> By pulling away from our ordinary self-centered mode of being (where in our attempts to grasp the self, we get caught in its grasp), and by taking hold of things where things have a hold of themselves, so do we revert to the "middle" of things themselves.[26]

The effort here is to realize not only the interconnectedness of all phenomena but also their beauty and integrity. Philosophers in the West since ancient times have referred to the "light of reason" whereby the human mind is trained on objects, like a beam or a searchlight, to pluck them out of the "darkness" of ignorance and expose them to knowledge and scrutiny. But Nishitani wants us to recognize that it is not our wonderful and *exclusively human reason* that makes this possible but the "light of each and every thing." To give all the credit to our reason is, indirectly, to elevate man again to the "center" of things and neglect the principle that the most true centering is when you no longer try to single and separate out of everything else something you have arbitrarily designated as their center.

---

[23] *Religion and Nothingness,* p. 123.

[24] *Religion and Nothingness,* p. 137.

[25] Trans. by the author.

[26] *Religion and Nothingness,* p. 140.

In this Nishitani seems to borrow an important principle expressed in a basic metaphor used in the *Avataṁsaka-sūtra* or Wreath-Garland Sutra, an important Mahayana text.[27] It is called the metaphor of Indra's Net, in which Indra, a great god in the Indian tradition, is said to have in his heavenly kingdom a vast net that stretches out in all directions. Actually it is stretched out infinitely and is, therefore, itself equal to the universe. The significant thing about it, however, is that in each of the "eyes" in the mesh of this cosmic-sized net there hangs a precious jewel and these too are infinite in number. Each is glittering and shimmering. But upon close inspection one finds that each jewel there reflects the multitude of other glittering jewels; that is, the light of all is mirrored in each and all. In addition, there is no one jewel in that vast net that could possibly be singled out as having special or central importance. The beauty and majesty of the universe lies not in the elevation of one jewel to a preeminent position or role but in the mutual and unhindered interreflection and co-illumination achieved by the vast array of particular gems. This, of course, is a metaphor for Buddhism's teachings of no ātman; it also implies co-dependent origination.

Nishitani, it seems, has not only grounded his philosophy in classical Buddhism but has shaped it until it has become a critique of the modern mind and its peculiar tendency to elevate man's reason to some kind of status in the universe— the unquestioned center around which everything else is thought to swirl as the things that alone have to be questioned and probed. This image of a centralized human intellect is deeply lodged in Western patterns of thinking but is inconsistent with the portrait of reality expressed in the metaphor of Indra's net; it is especially put in difficulty when subjected to the scrutiny of Nishitani's critique.

But Nishitani does not overlook the fact that getting to this realization is far from easy. In fact, it is in this area that he insists upon the need for what in Zen has often been called the Great Doubt. He cites a Buddhist text that advises:

> You must doubt deeply . . . gathering together in yourself all the strength that is in you, without aiming at anything or expecting anything in advance, without even intending to be enlightened and without even intending not to be enlightened . . . becoming completely like a dead man, unaware even of the presence of your own person. Become yourself, through and through, a great mass of doubt. Then there will be a moment, all of a sudden, at which you emerge into a transcendence called the Great Enlightenment, as if you had awoken from a great dream, or as if, having been completely dead, you had suddenly revived.[28]

Doubt, of course, has been a method much used in science and philosophy; Descartes (1596-1650) championed its value. But that doubt, when compared with the

[27] Francis H. Cook, *Hua-yen Buddhism: The Jewel Net of Indra* (University Park, Pa., and London: The Pennsylvania State University Press, 1977), p. 2.
[28] *Religion and Nothingness*, pp. 20-21.

Great Doubt, is tame, only on the surface of things. It never questions the power of human reason itself—and thus always keeps reason itself in a special category, central and protected. It is a doubt that is intellectual without being existential, and it is one that is unable to transform the doubter in any radical way. It is unlike the doubt that Buddhists, especially those in the Zen school, have called the Great Doubt. And the Great Doubt in this tradition is the key—a key that the doubter must pursue at great risk—to gain a grasp of reality. The process of getting this far can only be an existential one, not a merely intellectual construct. In fact, in this interpretation the Great Doubt is the essence of the Great Death, now understood not as the final parinirvāṇa of Śākyamuni but as the essence of his experience of nirvana. It is what happens at that moment when the fundamental doubt about all things, expressed mythically in the tale of Śākyamuni being subjected to the wiles of Māra, gives way to the great affirmation, the deep recognition of the co-dependent origination of all things.

While holding to the importance of a religious perspective—something he received, in part, from his teacher, Nishida—Nishitani sees as futile and wrongheaded any attempt to return simplemindedly to the mythologies of the past or a religious world view of the period before the rise of modern science. Science has changed our world, and Nishitani has spent much of his life struggling with the implications of this fact. In an essay entitled "Science and Zen," he writes of the impossibility of ever really going back to a world in which man has again been placed in the *center* of things by a supposedly provident god, a world in which all of history is supposed also to unfold according to some divine plan. In fact, if the truth be told, we seem to be living in a somewhat unusual corner of a vast universe—unusual simply in the sense that it happens to be a part of the universe that is hospitable for biological life and for the life of human beings. Outside of this special "greenhouse" in which we live, there is great heat and great cold, conditions that are totally "natural" and at the same time totally inhospitable for us. Unless we carry our "greenhouse" conditions with us into space, the universe as a whole would be totally indifferent to our delicate constitution, our special needs, and even our "special" nature. Out there, just by virtue of being "natural," the universe would literally kill us—without any malevolence toward us whatsoever. This, according to Nishitani, is the nature of the universe as revealed by modern science, and in this science happens to be accurate.

> The image of the universe it sees is wholly exempt from the restriction of being an environment for man and is not in any sense man-created.[29]

This leads Nishitani to be, in fact, a critic of mythological and other "extraneous" elements that have in his view crept into Buddhism over many centuries. Moreover, he would seem to be standing directly within the Buddhist tradition in not feeling

---

[29] Keiji Nishitani, "Science and Zen," in *The Buddha Eye*, p. 133.

any need to locate, discover, or place a god or gods in this universe. In other words, he can insist upon the importance of religion without that of deity.

This is not to say, however, that he wishes to identify his position simply with that of a science that has become increasingly mechanistic in the twentieth century. He sees the need for pushing science too in the direction of recognizing the significance of the vision of the universe as structured by śunyatā. It is this universe, he insists, that can be seen anew as the "field of emptiness"—as long as a person is ready to make a great change of perspective.

> Such a dimension of bottomlessness can only open up in a religious existence that accepts the universe as a field for self-abandonment and for throwing away one's life; it can open only through the Great Death.[30]

And this, as things turn out, happens at the same time to be the entry point for the Great Affirmation.

---

[30] *Religion and Nothingness*, p. 126.

6

the buddha: models and rituals

This is the place to clarify and expand on what is meant by the term "Buddha" when Buddhists make their customary claim to be taking refuge in the Buddha, the dharma, and the sangha. It is also the place to describe worship in the context of Buddhism. Fortunately these two projects come together well. We will, however, have to point out exactly why the term "worship" is not always appropriate in Buddhism even though there is, in fact, a good deal of ritual activity there.

Westerners often simply assume that when Buddhists use the word "Buddha" they mean something that is the equivalent of what Christians and many Jews mean when they refer to God; they also assume, then, that Buddhists can be expected to be "worshippers of Buddha." This assumption can quite easily lead to a number of interconnected problems in understanding Buddhism, even though the non-Buddhist may have every intention of trying to get a grasp on Buddhism's teachings. This, then, is a good place to try to clear these problems away. But to do so we have to begin by noticing that the views of Buddhists will, at least at first sight, seem somewhat complex and complicated. This, at least in part, is because Buddhism in its long history has responded to quite a variety of cultures.

We can begin with the fact that, although Buddhism arose in India and is deeply imprinted by Indian cultures, it arose in a period of religious and philosophical ferment there. Buddhism began, moreover, as something of a maverick within Indian society. Therefore, although it is Indian, Buddhism was at the same time atypical; in fact, it later came to be classified as one of the types of Indian thinking that is officially "unorthodox." This opinion came into being primarily because Buddhists did not accept the Vedas, India's oldest religious ritual texts, as sacred scripture. The point of noticing this is that even from its earliest days, Buddhism was part of Indian culture but part of it in a slightly strange way. Ever since that time, then, there had been an element of tension between those forces, on the one hand, that would pressure Buddhism in the direction of being different and unique within Indian culture and those, on the other, that would try to pull it back to become again completely a part of general Indian thinking. (Some, in fact, conclude that it was the victory of the latter set of pressures that led later to the virtual demise of Buddhism as a separate philosophy later in Indian history.) This tension is reflected in the way—or, more precisely, the ways—in which Buddhists think about deity.

It seems quite clear that, according to the teaching of Śākyamuni, the term "Buddha" itself, which simply means "enlightened one," most appropriately is applied to human beings. This is because in Śākyamuni's own experience the perfection of enlightenment did not entail any departure on his part from the human species into which he had been born and in which he had fulfilled all the requirements to reach that perfection. In other words, his perfection was the perfection of his *human* nature; it did not mean that by his enlightenment he had gotten elevated to some category that was divine or suprahuman in any sense.

For many Buddhists, this is not in any sense a cause for disappointment; they would not have it otherwise. The exact nature of the way Buddhists reason about this deserves to be followed closely. They figure that, since Śākyamuni became the Buddha while still a human being, this indicates that getting to be born as a human being is itself a remarkable, special, and even wonderful event—in fact even a relatively rare one in the total economy of births that take place within the universe. The *number* of other beings, especially if microscopic ones are included, is far greater than that of humans—even on the overpopulated earth of the twentieth century. After all, they argue, how many thousands of lifetimes in species lower than that of the human did it require for us to reach this present birth as a human?!! They go on to insist that, therefore, this achievement should not be wasted.

Since Śākyamuni became a Buddha while being at the same time a man, there is an important sense in which being a human being is the highest possible privilege. Getting to be the Buddha, the most enlightened of beings, did not involve any effort or activity on the part of the gods to bring him to that point; none of them had to be incarnated in human form in order to bring salvation to Śākyamuni. It did not even entail any revelation of information from the realm of the gods—by angels or any other means. That is to say, the entire "salvation"—if enlightenment may be called a kind of "salvation"—of Śākyamuni took place while he remained in the same human category into which he had been born as an infant. His perfection was comprised of the development of his highest potentialities as a human being. This is a basic tenet of the Buddhist dharma in many Buddhist scriptures.

It does not, however, lead to the conclusion that all Buddhists are atheists who deny the existence of gods. In fact, at the time that Śākyamuni lived, the existence of multiple deities was almost universally believed in India. Although there were some thinkers in his day who claimed that it was necessary to deny categorically that gods existed, Śākyamuni did not go that far; his dharma left it up to individuals whether or not they wanted to believe in the existence of gods as such. In other words, members of the Buddhist sangha were at liberty to either believe or not believe in the existence of gods.

This is to say that this question was not considered to be one of crucial importance to Śākyamuni and the early sangha. The point is that, even though gods may exist, they are not especially involved in the enlightenment or salvation of any of us who are human beings. In addition, in Buddhism the question of our enlightenment is *the* single most important question of our existence and is regarded as the most fundamental religious problem for man. Therefore, since Buddhism teaches that the process of enlightenment for human beings is one in which only human beings are needed and involved, it follows logically that in Buddhism gods—even though they may exist—have no special *religious* role to play for man. The gods, if they exist, may be useful, but useful for less important, less ultimate, affairs. As odd as this may sound to persons who live in the Western traditions, it is fair to say that in Buddhism the question of deity is downgraded to the status of something that is not necessarily among the most important religious questions facing man.

When many Buddhists, then, try to think of what is "the highest" or the ideal form of existence, they do so in line with the foregoing. It does not occur to them to think of gods as other than unusually powerful beings—superior to humans in powers they can exercise but not necessarily more moral or more equipped to reach Buddha-hood. In fact, when they portray the activities of deities, the Buddhist scriptures are like most of those in the world inasmuch as gods are depicted as themselves swayed by emotions and passions. Even though they are gods and sometimes capable of superhuman feats, they still are apt to be fearful, full of desires, and even jealous of their own prerogatives. One of the Pali scriptures of the Theravada tradition says the following in an address to those of the Buddhist clergy aspiring to enlightenment:

> [Even] the leader of the gods, O priests, was not free from passion, was not free from hatred, was not free from infatuation. But that priest, O priests, who is a saint, who has lost all depravity, who has led the holy life, who has done what it behooved him to do, who has laid aside the burden, who has achieved the supreme good . . . is free from passion, is free from hatred, is free from infatuation.[1]

Here the contrast is clear: the gods are still subject to the laws of karma and are still paying the price for their own willful misdeeds in the past. The enlightened Buddhist monk or priest, by contrast, is free from karma and, since this in the Indian

---

[1] *Anguttara-Nikāya,* in Henry Clarke Warren, *Buddhism in Translations* (Cambridge, Mass.: Harvard University Press, 1896, and reprinted New York: Atheneum, 1969), pp. 424-425.

context is essentially the meaning of "salvation," is now beyond the need of any further salvation.

Since the gods, therefore, are still looking for a "way out" of their own predicament, it is logical for them to look to the Buddhist wise man for advice. Some Buddhist texts, especially Mahayana texts, include mention of large numbers of gods who join in along with other beings to listen to the sermons of the Buddha. But the human teacher of the gods need not even be portrayed as resplendent. According to the line of reasoning just suggested, the gods do themselves a favor when they stop to listen in while a simple, poor, but enlightened, mendicant is talking about the dharma. Even a person of the laity, if he or she has wisdom and knowledge of the Middle Path, deserves the respect and attentive ear of the gods.

The non-Buddhist might then legitimately ask, if God or the gods are not important agents or forces in enlightenment, the most important religious activity, what can possibly be the meaning and value of the many forms of ritual in which Buddhists engage? For certainly Buddhists *do* perform rituals and engage in activities that seem very much like the things called "worship" in Western contexts. Is it not inconsistent for Buddhists to claim that the gods are unnecessary for the attainment of real religious goals and then spend much of their time and energies in what can only be called worship activities?

These are excellent questions. Many Buddhists would answer them by claiming that in their view at least there is no inconsistency here. This is because when the Buddhist bows before another human being or even prostrates himself in front of an icon representing the Buddha or a bodhisattva, this act is not the worship of an inherently and always superior being but the expression of deepest respect for qualities and virtues that the worshiper recognizes in others and at the same time expects to attain himself or herself. It may be correct to call this "worship," but it is necessary to remember that this is worship carried out by someone on the path and directed toward someone else on that same path. In fact, that "someone else" may be that which the worshipper envisions himself or herself to become at some later stage of attainment. One scholar writes:

> Note that worship means to remember the qualities of the Buddha and to confirm one's intention to follow his path. This is not worship of a deity.[2]

Another way of looking at this is to note that in Buddhism the activity of worship has no stopping point. Even Śākyamuni Buddha, the highest being who lived within the time and space that is relatively close to us, worshipped Buddhas in the more distant past who had been his teachers and spiritual benefactors. This is the corollary of what in Chapter 1 we called the "open ends of history"; here we might call it the "open-endedness of worship" in Buddhism. It is merely the position that, since the act of worshipping is spiritually a very healthy activity for the

---

[2] Michael Carrithers, *The Forest Monks of Sri Lanka: An Anthropological and Historical Study* (Delhi: Oxford University Press, 1983), p. 77.

one who engages in it, even the powerful and enlightened beings will wish, and in-deed feel privileged, to do it. Therefore, according to the sutras, not only the gods come to worship the Buddha but the Buddha himself is always ready and happy to have the opportunity to worship another Buddha. There is no one worshipped who is not also a worshipper. This highly praised and prized activity never comes to a point where some being is the *final object* and recipient of worship. And this, of course, fits in perfectly with the Buddhist refusal to think of any single being as the creator or progenitor of all other beings and forms of existence. It fits in with what we noticed was the metaphor of the universe as Indra's net, a vast complex of mu-tually reflecting gems, none of which had centrality or priority. In other words, worship as the Buddhists understand it, works best when it is reciprocal or runs in circles; since it is a good, it must be good for every one in the universe. No one in his or her right mind would want to be the recipient of it without at the same time having the opportunity to engage in the worship of others.

One way of phrasing this, and a way especially prized in the Mahayana tradi-tion, is in the teaching of śunyatā or emptiness. Ju-ching, the Chinese teacher of the Japanese Zen master Dōgen in the thirteenth century, told him: "The nature of both the worshipping and the worshipped is void."[3] Here again the term "void" or "emptiness" has its specifically Buddhist sense, that is, as something that is in-finitely related to all other things, even to the extent of recognizing in them some-thing worthy of being worshipped. "Emptiness" here need not be so mysterious; it points to the fact that in worship, there should be no walls, no metaphysical limits. Literally it is an activity that is *end*-less. Every object of worship is itself in some way or another engaged in worship. Every Buddhist takes refuge in the Buddha, but every Buddha takes refuge in other Buddhas—perhaps even in the Bud-dha taking refuge in him or her. The teaching of "emptiness" is said to run in circles in this fashion, but these are considered to be very beneficial circles that at the same time articulate and are in harmony with the structure of the universe.

It is important to remember, however, that these are subtle and often diffi-cult ways of looking at things, not just for modern Westerners but also for Indians of Śākyamuni's own day. This is clear from the evidence of the tension referred to at the beginning of this section: tension, that is, between the centrifugal force that tried to push Buddhism out in the direction of being a uniquely different teaching in Indian culture and the centripetal one that tried to pull it back again into con-formity with the mainline or orthodox assumptions of Indian religious culture. This tension is seen in some of the earliest Buddhist scriptures and, in fact, shows up even in the early stories about the birth of Śākyamuni. The problem is this: according to what we have written thus far, Śākyamuni is understood to have been an ordinary human being. We might assume, then, that his birth was very much like that of the rest of us, involving the usual sexual union of his father and his mother and his entry into the world through his mother's birth canal.

---

[3] James Takeshi Kodera, *Dōgen's Formative Years in China: An Historical Study and An-notated Translations of the Hokyō-ki* (London: Routledge & Kegan Paul, 1980), p. 122.

Calligraphy by Shin'ichi Hisamatsu

Such, however, is not the way the Buddhist scriptures portray it. The account in later texts, such as the Jākata tales, is clearly fabulous, embellished by all kinds of miraculous events. These events include his entry into his mother by way of a dream, an exit through her side, his ability to stand up, make profound statements immediately after being born, and the like. It is interesting to note that other texts in the Pali tradition, texts that were composed *earlier* than the Jātakas, are much less fabulous and mythological. But the important point is that even those Pali texts, from a stratum of scriptures that ordinarily is quite sober-minded and down-to-earth about many things, presents the Buddha-to-be as deliberately and consciously choosing to enter his mother's womb and then making his entry into the world "stainlessly" and without any "defilement by watery matter, blood, mucous, or other impurity." Moreover, they make no mention of a sexual union on the part of his parents and leave the impression at least that this was a conception for which such an act was unnecessary. Therefore, although the later texts are more fabulous than the earlier ones, even the early ones hint that this was a birth without any impurities and without the need for sex on the part of the infant's parents. The question then arises, at least in our minds today: What are we to make of this emphasis upon this rather unusual manner of coming into our world?

Anthropologists can often be very helpful in understanding things like this. At least Gananath Obeyesekere provides an explanation that rings true. He points out that, at least in cultures heavily influenced by India, it is one of the hallmarks of a figure who is understood to be a deity that he will be thought of as having avoided contact with impure substances: bodily secretions and exuviae that are viewed as especially polluting. This applies, of course, to the liquids and substances associated with menstruation, sexual intercourse, elimination, and childbirth. To summarize Obeyesekere's fascinating analysis, we can see from the texts that the Buddhists who wrote them were in a bind. On one hand, they needed to demonstrate, as discussed, that Śākyamuni was born as a human being since that had been clear to those who had known him and was an important part of his own teaching about himself. On the other hand, however, to present him in a way that was really acceptable within the religious and social expectations of Indian culture, his birth had to be depicted as a coming into this world without contact with any of the polluting liquid substances invariably connected with conception and birth.[4]

To this we might add the following. The earlier texts of Buddhism that wanted to keep Śākyamuni as close as possible to what we know is the ordinary course of human conception and birth tried to solve this problem with a light touch; they simply remained silent about his conception and said that his birth, although through the womb, was somehow "stainless." The reader or listener was free to speculate about what concretely that "stainlessness" might have involved. Later, more extravagant texts went much farther and left much less to the imagination; they presented him as conceived when his mother dreamed of an elephant, as being born through her side rather than the wet, "polluting" birth canal, and even as standing up on two feet immediately after being born in order to proclaim his own *special* nature. Clearly the pressure of Indian cultural expectations was at work on those writing these texts; the later ones, such as the Jātakas, present a Buddha who has become more and more like the divine beings adulated in India. In that sense at least the texts increasingly pictured him with characteristics long associated with the "gods," even though the Buddhist tradition itself at this point included his own statements to the effect that he neither wanted nor needed respect as anything other than a human among other humans.

We have here noted the cultural role of pollution and its avoidance in Indian religious culture. Certainly this has traditionally been very important in India, but at least some aspects of it have been shared by other cultures as well;[5] in Christian cultures, too, there exists the belief that the incarnation of Jesus Christ was accompanied by the miracle of a Virgin birth—something quite similar to the Indian assumption that the births of gods into this world are most properly ones for which the ordinary sexual union between a man and woman is not only not needed but, in fact, undesirable if the god's divine nature and purity are to be maintained. Although probably Indian culture was more explicit than most in relating the notion of virgin birth to that of pollution through contact with body fluids, similar ideas are present in other cultures as well. And in still other cultures, even though it may

---

[4] Gananath Obeyesekere, "The Goddess Pattini and the Lord Buddha: Notes on the Myth of the Birth of the Deity," *Social Compass,* Vol. 20, no. 2 (1973), 217-229.

[5] See Mary Douglas, *Purity and Danger: An Analysis of Concepts of Pollution and Taboo* (Baltimore: Penguin Books, 1970).

not have been there from the beginning, it was something that people could grasp with relative ease.

We ought not be surprised, then, when we see that some aspects of this mythologized account of Śākyamuni's birth were not just quirks of Indian culture but had, in fact, considerable appeal even outside of India—in the very different cultures of China and Japan, for instance. Perhaps this is because precisely at the time when they accepted Buddhism, many people in these cultures were openly fascinated and even enthralled with things that had their origins in India. But more probably it is because, at least to some extent, there is a more general human fascination with deity figures and the captivating stories that can be told about the special circumstances of their births and lives. And this, of course, is to note that, in spite of all that was said earlier in this section about the total humanity of the Buddha, Buddhists have not always and everywhere, therefore, refrained from pushing him, at least in their minds, farther and farther into a category of very special humanity. And from there he could easily come to be considered "divine."

The rich research and findings of anthropologists are quite clear about this. Even in Theravada cultures such as that of Sri Lanka, some monks in their monasteries may be scrupulously insistent that Buddha was a human being and never anything other than a human. They may even, as in some instances, refuse to have images of the Buddha in their compounds so that there will be no misunderstanding of this point. But other monks and especially the general population, the laity, will have a respect for Buddha-hood that quite easily becomes a form of worship. The process of this elevation is no doubt gradual and may be almost imperceptible. Who exactly can say what is happening in the minds and hearts of the pious people? Who can detect at what point their thinking about the Buddha as a human has become thinking about him as having very special, virtually unique, attributes? And then where exactly is the line between this and what becomes in fact a complete apotheosis of him as a god?

Although we cannot draw the lines, we can detect places where a struggle has taken place because of this underlying tension within the tradition. Moreover, it occurred not only in the cultures of the Theravada tradition but also in those of the Mahayana. The development of Mahayana, especially in East Asia, was confronted with an immense problem. Many people were fascinated with the concept of the Buddha as very special, a cosmic being who, while not subject to passions of anger and jealousy, was replete with compassion, wisdom, and composure. On the other hand, the tendency to elevate him to a status far beyond that of ordinary mortals put in jeopardy the sutras' claim that he was a human, not a god. The more the vision of him was one of a holy being, the more it emphasized his purity and existence in the realm of nirvana far from this world.

But the Indian philosopher Nāgārjuna and others had insisted that in Buddhism there is no nirvana apart from samsara, no realm of "purity" detached from the impurity in which ordinary mortals live their lives. Within the development of Buddhist philosophy in Mahayana there were thinkers who felt very uncomfortable with easy distinctions, often called "dualisms," between what is pure and impure, holy and profane, or what has Buddha-nature and what does not have it. In fact some thinkers regarded such discriminating activity as itself "impure."[6]

This had deep implications for how people were to think of the Buddha. Especially in the development of the Ch'an and Zen tradition in East Asia, there was a repeated and often strikingly insistent attempt to return to the conception of the Buddha as a mere human being. The masters of Ch'an were also masters at making this point vivid and did so in the idiom of China. It is against the background of what they took to be too much adulation of a Buddha divinized and removed from ordinary human beings that Ch'an teachers used language and gestures that were iconoclastic.

> **Monk** : *Master, what is the Buddha?*
> **Master** : *Three pounds of flax!*

Or, in order to make the point so strong that no one would miss it, their religious language became scatological:

> **Monk** : *Master, what is the Buddha?*
> **Master** : *The shit-stick! [used for cleansing at that time in China because of the preciousness of paper]*

It was also part of what lay behind the seemingly irreverent way in which the Japanese master Ikkyū dedicated a new icon of the Buddha by urinating on it—the narrative included in our opening chapter. The point of this, of course, is not to engage in irreverence and iconoclasm for its own sake. Some teachers have said that in Buddhism iconoclasm is only legitimate and right after one has truly learned the value and real importance of the icon. Until that point it is showy, ego inflating, and futile. The point of the Zen masters' irreverent and sometimes outrageous behavior was really to wean their disciples away from the notion that the Buddha is somewhere outside of those students themselves, in some thing made out of gold and wood on an altar, or in a person who lived many centuries ago and has his words written down in sacred books, or in the student's own personal master as a projection of everything the student wants himself to be.

A THERAVADA MONASTERY

Visitors to the lands where Theravada Buddhism remains strong today, such as Sri Lanka, Burma, and Thailand, have often been struck by a strange and puzzling incongruity. On the one hand, virtually all the people of those countries consider themselves Buddhists and show, in fact, virtually no mental reservation about their

---

[6] Masao Abe, "The Idea of Purity in Mahayana Buddhism," in *Zen and Western Thought*, ed. by William LaFleur (Honolulu: University of Hawaii Press, 1985), pp. 216–222.

acceptance of the truth of the Buddhist dharma. At the same time large numbers of the laity in these countries pay their respects at shrines dedicated to deities that are Hindu in origin and seem to be unconnected to Buddhism. Moreover, even when they go to Buddhist temples, their actions there are primarily cultic; those actions seem directed to the icons of the Buddha there. They bow, burn incense, or place flowers before these images. Especially in the villages, there will be monks who live in village temples and perform largely ceremonial functions for the laity. They are much less strict than the true ascetics.

> The village monk is always vulnerable to criticism on the basis of Vinaya, for however good he may be in comparison with other villagers, he is still likely to be out of touch with most of the monastic rules.[7]

Such village monks not only are somewhat looser in their keeping of the traditional vinaya rules, they also perform primarily cultic functions. They are, that is, largely priests performing the rituals required by the laity. They are officiants in rites of worship.

By contrast, there are other Buddhist monks in these same Theravada countries who keep themselves well removed from most of these cultic activities. These perform virtually no rituals whatsoever. This difference between the ritual-observing laity and its priests, on the one hand, and those monks who have little or nothing to do with such activities, on the other, has sometimes led Western or Western-trained anthropologists to come to the conclusion that in these countries, there really are two *separate* religious systems that exist side by side, almost without touching one another. One system embraces the activities of the strict monks: meditation, the study of the Pali texts of the tradition, and the occasional preaching of the dharma to the laity. The other system is that of the laity and their ritual-officiant priests in the villages: the worship of a wide variety of deities and Buddha figures that have come to function in the same way as deities. Some scholars have even gone on to suggest that it is the latter that is the deeply entrenched religion and, therefore, even the *real* religion of the people of these lands. By contrast, the strict monk's ideals and practices are a superficial overlay on the culture. The term sometimes used to describe the latter is "veneer," that is, something that makes things look highly polished but remains, when all is said and done, something only on the surface of things.

Of course, this raises important and interesting questions about the relationship between Buddhism and culture, questions that ought not be dismissed and cannot be answered simply. However, part of the reason why these two systems seem to exist side by side in Theravada countries must have to do with the fact that virtually everyone there—whether monk or layperson—sees life as, in fact, a sequence of lives. Scholars who have conducted interviews have found that for all Theravada Buddhists, monk and layperson alike, the ultimate goal of existence is

---

[7] Carrithers, *The Forest Monks of Sri Lanka*, p. 106.

to attain nirvana. On this point at least, there is very little difference between the stated goals of the monks and the laity.

But an ultimate goal may lie far in the future—in fact it may lie many lives away! This means that for many people in these cultures the arrival at that ultimate goal is not at all within easy reach. A number of lives have to be lived in between this one and that future life that will be the entry into nirvana. In these interim lives, the person involved will have to purify himself or herself and gradually make an ascent toward the long-range goal. For the monk who has both cut himself off from the householder's livelihood and by becoming a strict monastic is now devoting nearly twenty-four hours a day in order to enter nirvana, that goal is—at least comparatively—within sight; those who are practicing their Buddhism with this level of concentration are expecting to reach it relatively soon. But for the layperson and even for the village monk serving as a ritualist, by contrast, nirvana is still very far off. He or she believes, however, that the accumulation of meritorious deeds will enable him or her to gain rebirth later as someone able to practice the Middle Path intensively and at that point the ultimate goal of nirvana will finally be within sight.

But in the interim there are lots of objectives and things that, even though they are not nirvana, are certainly desirable.[8] It is for reaching these objectives that attention to the various kinds of deities and even to the Buddha as a kind of god figure is considered beneficial. Cultic attention to the various deity figures may do much, at least according to these laypersons, to make crops grow, businesses prosper, infertile couples fertile, and childbirth safe. The gods may not give access to nirvana—the ultimate religious goal—but they are thought beneficial to give a person many of the things that make this life good and prosperous. Therefore, the two systems that at first sight seemed so different and unrelated are, at least according to some observers, really "complementary and interdependent."[9]

To the careful observer, this relationship is expressed even in architecture. They claim that architectural arrangements can serve as a concrete and visually powerful pattern of symbols in religion. We can, in fact, learn a great deal about Theravada Buddhism if we know how to look carefully at its buildings and the physical layout of the compounds of its monasteries. One anthropologist, Jacques Maquet, made a detailed and fascinating study of the plan and uses of the Kanduboda monastery in Sri Lanka, a monastery that had been built on land cleared away from a coconut plantation in 1956. This monastery was special in that it was founded in 1956, the year that in Buddhist countries was widely celebrated as the twenty-five hundredth anniversary of the death or full liberation of Śākyamuni.

[8] Melford E. Spiro differentiates the penultimate goal as Buddhism for which karma is still important and the ultimate one as that for which nirvana is such; see his *Buddhism and Society: A Great Tradition and Its Burmese Vicissitudes* (New York: Harper & Row, 1970).

[9] Hans-Dieter Evers, "Buddha and the Seven Gods: The Dual Organization of a Temple in Central Ceylon," *Journal of Asian Studies,* Vol. 27, no. 3 (May 1968), 541.

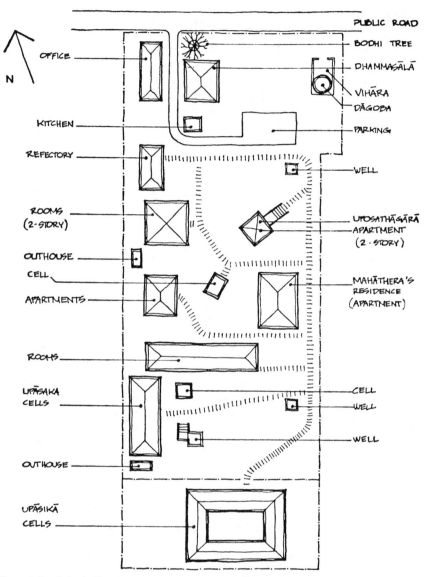

PUBLIC ROAD
BODHI TREE
OFFICE
N
DHAMMASĀLĀ
VIHĀRA
DĀGOBA
KITCHEN
PARKING
REFECTORY
WELL
ROOMS
(2-STORY)
UPOSATHĀGĀRĀ
APARTMENT
(2-STORY)
OUTHOUSE
CELL
APARTMENTS
MAHĀTHERA'S
RESIDENCE
(APARTMENT)
ROOMS
UPĀSAKA
CELLS
CELL
WELL
WELL
OUTHOUSE
UPĀSIKĀ
CELLS

Plan of Kanduboda Monastery

(This date is due to a traditional method of reckoning that is slightly different from those generally accepted by scholars today. It places the death of Śākyamuni at 544 B.C.E.) Raising the funds to construct Kanduboda had been the responsibility of a group of laymen since, according to Buddhist rules, monks themselves are not supposed to handle or be concerned with money. Like all monasteries in Theravada countries, food for the monks is supplied daily by pious laypersons; in the case of

Kanduboda, however, it is brought in daily on a scheduled basis from groups of laity from a very wide geographical area. Jacques Maquet's research on the plan of this monastery is what he calls the study of its "expressive space"; it provides an aperture through which we can see the interrelationship of the various elements within such a compound and, in the process, learn much about the Theravada.

The plan of the monastery deserves close inspection.[10] There is a fence around the whole of it, but upon entering the compound from the public road on the north side, one enters initially a part, roughly one-fourth, that is public and open to the laity. It includes the office where the donations are received; a kitchen where the already cooked food is warmed up again for the monks; a symbolic bodhi tree that memorializes the one at Bodh Gaya, India, where Śākyamuni was enlightened; a preaching hall (*dhammasālā*); and a hall (*vihāra*) where an icon of the Buddha is kept. Maquet calls this entire area a "marginal" zone; it is not part of the area outside the fence and public road north of the compound but also not part of the inner area to the south, the place where the strict monastics live and practice. To that extent, this marginal area is neither a part of the impure and secular world outside nor is it yet fully inside the sacred compound where the really serious and dedicated practitioners of Buddhism live their exemplary, purified, lives according to the traditions and codes of the Theravada. The important point to note, however, is that it is in this *marginal* area where the icon of the Buddha is located and where the general public may enter in order to bow in the presence of this image; Maquet notes that it is significant that the places of worship are located here rather than in the inner enclosure, the monastery in the strict sense. Further the point should not be missed that those who live inside the more inner compound do *not* have to come out into this area or perform activities of worship there. In fact, its placement exactly at this point suggests that worship as such is considered valuable for the laity but unimportant and even unnecessary for those who have gone "beyond" the need for it, that is, those living and practicing their Buddhism within the more inner portion of the compound. The point, according to Maquet, is that this is a visual, spatially expressed statement: "devotional practices are good for laymen, and should be irrelevant for monks."[11]

South of this marginal portion then lies the area where the more serious monastics live and carry on their meditations. The best way to follow Maquet's careful diagram is to imagine oneself leaving the marginal zone and walking on the concrete walkways that begin there. If one were a woman, she could follow the walkway that runs toward the eastside fence, make a turn at the well, and then go directly south along that fence, pass through another fence that runs east-west, and go into the rectangular group of *upāsikā* cells. These are the quarters not of nuns,

---

[10] The information and analysis in this section are from Jacques Maquet, "Expressive Space and Theravāda Values: A Meditation Monastery in Sri Lanka," *Ethos*, Vol. 3, no. 1 (Spring 1975), 1–21. I follow Maquet here in using Pali rather than Sanskrit terms for this discussion.

[11] Maquet, "Expressive Space," p. 7.

who in the twentieth century no longer exist in Sri Lanka, but of women disciples (upāsikā) who have taken the vows of specially dedicated laypersons and may remain here even for life. Those who are permanently there will be tonsured and also wear robes like monks; but among them there will also be untonsured women who wear white garments and stay only for a while. An important point to note is that their space and the building where they live and practice meditation are sharply separated, even by an additional fence, from that of the males on the compound; the understanding is that those on the path to nirvana will want to avoid every kind of sexual enticement and even the chance, unintended contact between men and women. Moreover, the separation of the upāsikā cells from the main compound and the fact that even the tonsured women who spend their whole lives there cannot officially today become nuns in Sri Lanka suggests that their status is subordinate to that of the males there. Space and how it is used are, after all, articulate.

The central and largest area of the compound is for the males who are serious practitioners at Kanduboda. Maquet notes that there are three types of buildings here and that status is clearly indicated by the kind of building one is in. They differ in size and degree of comfort. The most senior monks (*thera*) and head of the monastery (*mahāthera*) live in furnished apartments that are not unlike those of well-to-do Sri Lankans who live outside in ordinary society. Those who have been ordained to full monkhood (junior *thera* and *bhikkhu*) occupy their own rooms that are simple but private. The novices who are aspirants for monkhood and laymen who are at the monastery temporarily for a period of meditation are both classified as lay (male) practitioners (*upāsaka*). Each of them occupies a cell in the building so designated. These cells are very austere: a cement bed with a mat, a low table, no window, a single light bulb hanging over the partition and serving two cells at the same time.

A similar kind of differentiation according to status is shown in the refectory or common dining room, the only place in the entire compound where the monks come together twice a day. Since by long-standing tradition in the Theravada no meals are to be eaten after noon each day, the eating of the cooked foods provided by the laity takes place at 6:30 A.M. and again at 11:30 A.M. Then there is no food again until the next morning—a way of insisting upon the monk's need to focus on meditation during all the other hours.

Since the novice in training at Kanduboda is physically present with his fellows only at mealtime and in addition spends only approximately fifteen minutes each day with his meditation teacher, Maquet calculates that this novice's time spent alone is about twenty-three out of twenty-four hours in each day. Maquet then goes on to summarize:

[All this] expresses perfectly the inward orientation of an intense and concentrated mental culture. It contributes also to the development of the one-pointedness of mind that is sought by the meditators. The world of sensory stimulations and of ego-attachments is beyond the monastery fences; between it and the *yogi* space, the inner enclosure provides another protection. Surrounded by concentric spaces of silence and quietness, the *yogi* is free to pursue his solitary quest for liberation.[12]

The important thing to note is that there is no common worship hall, as, for instance, can be found in most Catholic monasteries. Not only is there no place where the monastics and ordinary laity gather for worship, there is not even a place where the monastics themselves do so as a group. They ordinarily do not even enter the north end of the compound where the laity come from outside to worship at the shrine of the Buddha. At Kanduboda, at least, they perform no rituals for the laity; their lives are understood to be led in a full-time pursuit of the meditation and the nirvana that awaits them. Maquet notes that the absence of communal space in such a Theravada monastery is no accident.[13]

Perhaps another instructive contrast is that with the meditation hall of Ch'an or Zen monks in East Asia.[14] The term for this hall in Japanese is *zendō*, the word that has now come to be used in the West also to designate the primary meditation room of established Zen institutions. Whereas the Theravada monks traditionally meditated in private and individually—in cells, in thatched huts, in mountain caves, or the like—the practitioners of the Mahayana, including therefore those of Zen,

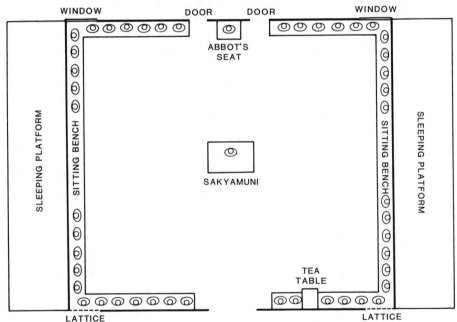

[12] Maquet, "Expressive Space," p. 19.

[13] Maquet, "Expressive Space," p. 13.

[14] Holmes Welch, *The Practice of Chinese Buddhism 1900–1950* (Cambridge, Mass.: Harvard University Press, 1967), p. 49. See also J. Prip-Møller, *Chinese Buddhist Monasteries* (London: Oxford University Press, 1937).

met together in large, common rooms for most of their meditations. This does not mean that solitary meditation was disallowed; certainly the exemplary story of Bodhidharma meditating in a Chinese cave for nine years is important. But the usual assumption has been that, except for rare individuals, most human beings profit greatly from the discipline of one another's presence. The regularized, timed meditations of Zen are strictly and collectively enforced; the violator cannot help but be noticed and corrected. Moreover, it is also a principle of the Mahayana—and one of their traditional objections to the "Small Vehicle" of which Theravada is a part—that nirvana, enlightenment, or salvation must be collectively, not just individually, pursued. The notion of the bodhisattva as one who postpones his own enlightenment until others can be enlightened as well expresses this. The interesting thing is that the difference in emphasis in the teaching here results in different nuances even in the way monastic compounds and buildings are organized. Jacques Maquet's point, then, that one can—at least if the eye is trained properly—"read" the teachings and its nuances even in the way buildings are laid out seems indisputable.

This is not to say, however, that the strict monastics of the Theravada are totally unrelated to the larger mass of people who never pass beyond the marginal zone of worship. The fact that they are known by all to be there, even if not often seen, has a spiritual and moral importance in such societies. Some students of Theravada Buddhism have stressed that the *exemplary* role of the strict practitioners is felt by those outside to give them encouragement in their own moral lives. Anthropologists and other students of the peoples living in these cultures have found among the laity virtually no resentment directed at the monks, no sense that their pursuit of mental and spiritual liberation is a selfish endeavor. On the contrary, they are very much admired and revered for the austerity of their disciplines. The level of purity attained by them in their daily lives is presently impossible for people living in ordinary society, but it is felt to be a strong and working example. Many laypersons in Theravada countries say that it is an important example to them merely to see a monk as he walks along a road—slowly, carefully, and meditatively. Whenever he becomes even visually present to others the monk can serve as model and illustration of the Buddhist path to nirvana. Even their strictest austerities are not the object of ridicule—as might be the case in Western societies—but things worthy of honor and the deepest respect. The point, of course, is that the strict monastics are only on the surface a separate society; on another level, all are deeply connected. With the passage through sufficient interim lives and the accumulation of sufficient merit the ordinary layperson too will someday—however far off—be at that very same place. When one's total religious "career" encompasses many lifetimes, there is a relationship between the here and now and later stages on the path to nirvana.

If this is so, there is a connection between the worship activities of the layperson before the image of Lord Buddha and the meditations of the monastic within the inner recesses of the compound. The former is a step toward the latter, even though those at the later stage do not have to go back to practice the earlier one again. Perhaps we might say that the worshippers in the marginal area are focusing their attention on a Buddha-hood that often seems, at least to their under-standing, concentrated and crystalized in the gold icon in front of them. As their education in the Middle Path progresses, especially through listening to the sermons of monks, they will more and more switch their focus to the Buddha-hood poten-tial within themselves. Those in the cells of the inner compound, however, have already passed over that boundary and are now devoting their full energies toward the realization of the Buddha-hood in their own bodies and minds. The former is a step toward the latter; the nuance of emphasis is different, but the line moves *clearly in one direction*. Although we do not ordinarily think of the meditations carried on by an individual and taking place in a separated cell as a form of "wor-ship" or "ritual," we probably should not limit our understanding of these words. There is a sense in which even these meditations are part of the *total* pattern of ritual activities in the context of Theravada Buddhism.

SESSHIN

Some might say that what American practitioners of Zen call a "sesshin" is a West-ern adaptation of a Japanese adaptation of a Chinese adaptation of an ancient Indian Buddhist period of concentrated meditation. But to think of it only as a series of adaptations places the accent on the cultural and historical *gaps* whereas, at least according to Zen teaching, to engage in this meditation allows a person to pass all the intervening space and time and do exactly *the same thing* that Śākya-muni did in order to become a Buddha. Sometimes the sesshin is referred to as a Zen "retreat," but that word can mislead. Unlike a "retreat," it does not include prayer in the usual sense; it will, however, include much more physical rigor than one would expect in a "spiritual" retreat. This means that it will also involve ac-tivities that, though ritualized, are intended to liberate the practitioner from his or her own routinized and unseeing way of looking at the world. The sesshin literally is a context in which even twentieth-century Westerners put themselves, both body and mind, in the same frame or mold that is said to have led to the paradigmatic event of Buddhism—the enlightenment of Śākyamuni in India more than twenty-five hundred years ago. But even if we call it a "ritual," it is not to be thought of as a remembrance or a faint shadow of the past. This would be to project Buddha-hood off into some place other than where we ourselves are. The stress in Zen, by contrast, is emphatically on the *present*, the practitioner's own Buddha-nature, and the fact that enlightenment is *already* present, not a goal standing somewhere off in the future.

What is described in the following pages could—and does—take place a num-ber of times each year in any one of the Zen communities that are found in the larger cities or rural settings of North America. Sesshins are also held in Europe, Australia, New Zealand, and Central and South America. Their location may be in buildings owned and specially equipped by a local Zen community or in homes or office buildings borrowed or rented for the time of the sesshin. In rural areas even barns, cleansed and adapted, have been used. Sometimes Catholic monks have invited Buddhists to come into their own monasteries to teach them the methods of Zen meditation; on such occasions, these Christians and Buddhists carry on sesshins together. This is possible because the person "doing" a sesshin does not have to think of himself or herself as a Buddhist; Christians and Jews who have sat in sesshin have found their own religious practices strengthened in this way.[15] Ideally, a sesshin will continue for a week or even for ten days, but, since the vast majority of Zen practitioners in the West are not monks but employed laypersons, the weekend sesshin has been a twentieth-century development in our own culture.

The word *sesshin* is the Japanese pronunciation of two Chinese characters that mean "to establish contact with the mind." As a word it suggests that sesshins aim to open up a degree of mind-body integration and awareness that differs from our usual experience. Zen masters are fond of saying that the mind ordinarily behaves like a monkey—restlessly and frantically climbing around in its cage. A sesshin aims to break the habits of this monkey mind by putting its owner in touch with the much calmer, clearer, deeper Buddha mind he or she already possesses. But the person doing a sesshin soon discovers that the body too is very much involved since, in Buddhism, the body and mind are generally understood to be closely linked and unified. This involvement of the body is also one reason why a sesshin is at least in some sense also ritualized activity. The person in a sesshin will spend most of his or her time there—often half the hours in a twenty-four-hour day—sitting on cushions in the zendō, the room where the practitioners meditate as a group. During the period of a sesshin, absolute silence is observed; with a few prescribed exceptions, no conversation is permitted among the participants.

Their principal activity there will be doing *zazen* or sitting meditation. Zazen begins with putting the body in order. Doing this may seem difficult at first because most of us not only have "monkey minds" but also fidgeting bodies. So this too has to be corrected. This is also the way to get the spine straight and the legs under you into what should become a firmly set, untottering basis. Usually a well-stuffed, hard cushion is placed under the buttocks. The sitter will want to feel well "rooted" but at the same time ready to rise quickly when "walking meditation" or other activities of bodily motion are called for. A more experienced sitter usually shows the first-timer how to take up the most appropriate of the four traditional postures for zazen: the full lotus, the half lotus, the Burmese, and what the Japanese call *seiza*.[16] The hands are then placed together; there are different ways of doing this, but a common one is by making a circle of fingers that touch lightly and are placed comfortably on the lap. Next comes control of the breath and greater consciousness of it. This too reaches directly back to actions prescribed by Śākyamuni:

---

[15] See Thomas Merton, *Zen and the Birds of Appetite* (New York: New Directions, 1968), and William Johnson, *Christian Zen* (New York: Harper & Row, 1971).

[16] [Rōshi] Robert Aitken, *Taking the Path of Zen* (San Francisco: North Point Press, 1982), pp. 18 ff., gives a fuller account.

[Let the person in meditation] sit down cross-legged, holding the body erect, and set his mindfulness alert. Mindful, let him inhale, mindful let him exhale. Whether he inhale a long breath, let him be conscious thereof; or whether he exhale a long breath, let him be conscious thereof . . .[17]

Becoming mindful of one's breathing, learning how to count the breaths with maximum attention, and the regulation of breathing into a pattern that is calm may take a fair amount of time and much more practice than one expects. The point, though, is that this too is the heart of the matter, not just a preliminary exercise or preparation.

You should not be tilted sideways, backwards, or forwards. You should be sitting straight up as if you were supporting the sky with your head. This is not just form or breathing. It expresses the key point of Buddhism. It is a perfect expression of your Buddha nature. If you want true understanding of Buddhism, you should practice this way. These forms are not a means of obtaining the right state of mind. To take this posture itself is the purpose of our practice.[18]

The point about this not being a *means* is crucial, especially in the tradition of Zen derived from the Japanese master Dōgen (1200–1253).

Somewhere in doing this the person in zazen will notice how much trouble he or she has keeping the monkey mind under control. While he or she is counting breaths, that mind will wander off, even without any outside stimulation. Daydreams, fantasies, intellectual games, even little jaunts of self-congratulation for doing the *zazen* will keep the mind scurrying around in its cage, doing anything and everything to spin the concentration off. The rapt attention to immediate reality will tend to slip away. But in Zen this is not considered a reason to feel that a mistake has been made or to incur some sense of guilt; the person who suddenly recognizes that his or her mind has begun to jump around again is encouraged simply to go back to being focused—again and again until the concentration builds and the mind becomes genuinely relaxed.

Also there will be pain, especially in the legs of persons not accustomed to the meditation positions. The periods of sitting will probably be somewhere around thirty minutes each, followed by five-minute periods of walking meditation. In a sesshin the daily schedule will begin at 3 or 4 A.M. and will continue until 9 P.M.; except for very brief restroom breaks and periods of silent, concentrated work (*samu*), usually in the kitchen or in the garden, almost all of the remaining time will be spent in the zendō.

---

[17] *Satipatthāna Sutta,* in T. W. and C. A. F. Rhys Davids, trans., *Dialogues of the Buddha,* Part II (London: Oxford University Press, 1910), p. 328.

[18] [Rōshi] Shunryu Suzuki, *Zen Mind, Beginner's Mind* (New York and Tokyo: Weatherhill, 1970), p. 26.

Full Lotus

Half Lotus

Seiza

Burmese

Four Meditation Postures *From* Taking the Path of Zen, *copyright © 1982 by Robert Aitken. Published by North Point Press and reprinted by permission. Drawing by Andrew Thomas.*

Ordinarily in our daily lives when we feel stiffness or discomfort due to body position, we simply move the affected limb into another place or position. But in zazen this would break the requirement of unmoving stillness. So the discomfort or pain has to be either endured or dealt with in some other way. Persons who are doing this kind of meditation for the first time will often become concerned about this pain and even complain about it; sometimes some change of position may be advised, but more likely he or she will be told that the pain in the legs is to be anticipated. (The fact of suffering, duḥkha, is, after all, the first noble truth.) They may also be told to "become one with the pain," advice that at first might seem insensitive but, in fact, can help considerably.

The exact daily schedule of a sesshin will differ slightly from one place to another, but most sesshins in North America will follow a schedule approximately like the following:

- 3:55 A.M.   wake up
- 4:20 A.M.   zazen (sitting in zendō)
- 6:50 A.M.   morning service (chanting and bowing)
- 7:20 A.M.   breakfast (on cushions in zendō)
- 8:00 A.M.   wash up and rest
- 9:00 A.M.   samu (work on location)
- 11:30 A.M.   zazen
- 12:00 noon   talk by roshi or teacher
- 12:30 P.M.   zazen
- 1:20 P.M.   noon service
- 1:30 P.M.   lunch (in zendō)
- 2:00 P.M.   rest
- 3:30 P.M.   zazen
- 5:20 P.M.   evening service
- 5:30 P.M.   snack and rest
- 7:00 P.M.   zazen
- 8:50 P.M.   closing service
- 9:30 P.M.   lights out and sleep

During the hours spent in the zendō there will be times when one of the senior teachers gives a short talk to everyone there. The times designated as "services" will be periods largely devoted to chanting short passages from the classical texts, the Heart Sutra (or *Hannya Shingyō*), for instance, (For a translation see pages 82–83) By far the majority of time, however, will be spent in meditation. With relatively little sleep, the impulse to daydream or drift off into actual slumber on the meditation cushion will appear quite naturally. This is why for many centuries the practitioners of Zen have seen value in having a monitor, a person who quietly and very, very slowly walks up and down the rows of silent meditators, watching to notice when the body shows that the mind has lost its concentration and focus. In the silence this monitor may at first seem threatening, but his or her role really is that of assistance, for instance, by quietly helping the sitter to achieve a better posture. Sometimes the monitor will also issue terse, sharp, strikingly loud words of encouragement to the entire body of sitters, reminding them, for instance, that the time of the sesshin will pass quickly and that the need for focused concentration is urgent. The monitor or the teacher in charge may borrow words from the Buddhist tradition such as that by Śākyamuni who is said to have told his disciples to practice with the concentration of a person who suddenly realizes that he or she has a fire blazing on top of the head, intensely eager to extinguish it by all means.

Keisaku—Encouragement *Eshin Nishimura and Bardwell L. Smith,* Unsui: A Diary of Zen Monastic Life. *Honolulu:* University of Hawaii Press, 1973, p. 31. Drawing by Giei Sato.

One other function of the monitor is to carry and use the *keisaku* (also called the *kyōsaku*), a lath of wood used to strike the shoulders of the sitters. The sudden, sharp sound of the keisaku being used in the midst of the silence of the meditation hall can be stimulating to the entire group, but its contact is especially so to the shoulders of the recipient. It will be used differently on different occasions—never, however, as an instrument of torture or vindictiveness. Nevertheless, it can be easily misunderstood by those who do not know it. Since it is peculiar to the Ch'an or Zen tradition, it is often misunderstood even by other Buddhists, not just by Westerners alone. In Bangkok a Theravada monk once told me he had heard about "the stick" used by Japanese Buddhists and went on to say that such a practice is contrary to the teachings of Śāyamuni. "Buddhism," he said with great emphasis, "is a path of gentleness, not an excuse for violence!" I hastened to tell him that in my own limited experience of the keisaku, it is a stimulus to practice, not a punishment and not really violent. Most frequently, it is used only when its application is deliberately requested by the meditator as the monitor passes his or her place; a silent bow will signal a request, and after it has been used, both persons will bow the gasshō bow to one another. Those with considerable experience with the keisaku—originally in East Asia but now in the West too—speak of it as direct and forceful benefit to the practice, something capable of helping both the body and the mind to focus on the hard work of meditation. Like many of the instruments of Zen, there is a difference between initial impression and actual function; in English the keisaku is often now called "the Encouragement," a term that fits its real purpose very well.

One of the other mystifying and seldom understood aspects of Zen practice, both to Westerners and to Asians, is the *kōan,* a form of practice that had its origins in China, was used in Japan primarily in the Rinzai school of Zen, and has been widely adopted into Western Zen as well. Many people have heard the words of kōans and suspect they may only be some kind of Zen joke or, at best, a conundrum with which to tease the mind. A classic example of a kōan is this:

A monk asked [Master] Chao-chou: "Who is Chao-chou?"
Chao-chou responded: "The east gate, the west gate, the south gate, the north gate."

A justly famous one coined by the Japanese master Hakuin (1685–1768) is this:

Everyone knows the sound of two hands clapping.
What is the sound of one hand clapping?

And perhaps the most famous of all—because it is frequently used as the first kōan tackled by a new practitioner of Zen—is this:

A monk asked Chao-chou: Does a dog have Buddha nature?
Chao-chou replied: *Mu.*

The correct use of a kōan in the Zen tradition, however, is not as a seemingly pointless bit of nonsense that brings a smile to the face and then is felt no more. A kōan such as that last one known as the "Mu kōan" is given in a context of great seriousness by a master or teacher to a student; it is anticipated that the latter will struggle with it and make it the focus of his or her meditation until it makes "sense"—not intellectual but personal, existential sense. Traditional and current teachers of Zen insist that the kōan is totally misunderstood if thought to be meaningless.[19] But the kōan is also misunderstood if taken to be something that the mind alone must crack open—merely like another difficult problem in mathematics or a difficult word to translate from one language into another. Such things, the teachers insist, have nothing to do with the kōan. Masao Abe takes note of something important, namely, that according to an old source, the word kōan is comprised of two parts:

the *kō* of *kōan* means sameness or ultimate equality that is beyond equality and inequality, and *an* refers to "keeping one's sphere [in the universe]."

---

[19] Aitken, *Taking the Path of Zen,* pp. 101 ff.

Kōan thus indicates the individuality of things' differences and the difference of things' sameness.[20]

Frequently, the person in meditation is told to "put the kōan" in the belly, not the mind. This suggests that it is to be worked on physically and existentially, not just as an intellectual problem. This difference is very important. Masao Abe has said that it is evidenced in the difference between the Western ideal of the intellectual and the Buddhist ideal of the Buddha. He says it shows up even in art. If the West's ideal is shown in Rodin's sculpture "The Thinker," a man sitting with his heavy head bent over and held up by his hand, that of Buddhism is shown in the images of the Buddha sitting squarely on the earth with his hands making a mudra in his lap. The center of gravity in the latter is in the very center of the body, not the "belly" in terms of digestive functions but what East Asians have often called the "vital center." It is this way of centering the body that is important in Zen meditation, in the plan for most Buddhist icons, and also in the practice of the so-called "martial arts" of China, Korea, and Japan.

As the Zen practitioner struggles with a kōan, he or she will go during the sesshin for formal interviews with the *rōshi,* the resident master or teacher. The purpose of this interview will be to have his or her understanding of the kōan checked. The nature of this interview deserves some attempt at a description, even though most of it will elude any such attempt. It begins in a very ritualized way: the person wanting to see the rōshi will have to join in a queue with others wanting to do the same. When his or her own time comes to go privately into the rōshi's interview room—usually set apart from the zendō in some way—it is proper to bow. This bow is not just the gasshō but a full prostration that is repeated three times. Then the kōan is repeated in this face-to-face encounter with the rōshi, who will be sitting perfectly still and silent. Then the rōshi will demand that the student give some proof of having penetrated the kōan or of having made progress in that direction. This might be verbal, but it might also be physical. It is the *spontaneous* demonstration of the enlightened mind that is what the rōshi will wish to see. Spontaneity that is planned cannot be spontaneous. Therefore, any mentally contrived show of spontaneity that is plotted in the mind of the student before entering the interview room will be seen through immediately by the rōshi. When the rōshi has determined that the interview is over, he simply rings a little bell. Then the student must bow again and depart immediately. The interview is over. The next person in the queue outside the rōshi's door will then enter his room.

---

[20] "Introduction," to Dōgen, "Shōbōgenzō Genjōkōan," trans. by Norman Waddell and Masao Abe, *The Eastern Buddhist,* n.s., Vol. 5, no. 2 (October 1972), 130. See also "Non-being and *Mu:* The Metaphysical Nature of Negativity in the East and West," in Abe, *Zen and Western Thought,* ed. William R. LaFleur (Honolulu: University of Hawaii Press, 1985).

Those moments of spontaneity—or, at least, hoped-for spontaneity—in the rōshi's room will seem to contrast with many other aspects of the sesshin, most of which will be preset and ritualized. Much of the week will appear, at least on the surface, to be an ongoing round of predetermined moves from the cushion to walking meditation to silent periods of work to meals that will be simple in what is eaten but unusually complex in form. Every moment of the day will seem scheduled, with virtually none of that which we usually call "free time." The week will have its pains, its crises of various types, and, it is hoped, also its progress in terms of getting some taste of Zen.

In addition to the wooden stick that some now call "the Encouragement," other forms of support will come from the short talks given in the zendō by the rōshi or his senior students. Different people may have different ideas about how slowly or quickly the week passes; time will begin to take on a different dimension. Important, however, will be the movement toward what is called *kenshō,* that experience in which a person has some fundamental insight into his or her own nature. Kenshō is not final or full enlightenment but a very important "glimpse," one that has been described in ecstatic terms by those who have chosen to write about it. Most Zen teachers, however, will tend to be fairly tight-lipped about their own kenshō since, while the experience is of fundamental importance, talk about it is not.

The final night of a sesshin is one in which the intensity of the practice perceptibly grows. The words of encouragement from the teacher will be words telling all to strive harder; students will be reminded that life is brief, that opportunities such as the present one are few and far between, and that one never knows if and when such a chance might occur again. Many of the participants in the sesshin will then choose to forego sleep so that they can spend the entire night doing meditation either in the zendō or some place out of doors. (In Japan where there is often a cemetery on the premises of a temple, such a place provides an ideal context for meditation during the final night of a sesshin. Buddhaghosa might prefer more vivid materials to do the "meditations on the foul," but the use of even a modern cemetery recapitulates Śākyamuni's experience.)

The end of a sesshin may be accompanied by mixed feelings. There is relief that the period of rigor, stiffness, and little sleep is over. Most people are happy to have the chance to take a long, uninterrupted sleep and to talk freely to others again. There is often a sense too that what at first seemed so onerous during the days of the sesshin began at least to some degree to seem natural. For many participants, the week will have turned out to have been very different from what they expected it to be—most often in a positive way. The pluses of the week may be measured by some in terms of distinct progress in realizing their original nature and by others in terms of learning how better to sit in zazen and how better to regulate their lives. Those who have a deep sense that they are still only beginners in this matter will often be reminded by others that, in the words of Rōshi Shunryu Suzuki

Rōshi, the beginner's mind is the Zen mind.[21] Probably not a few of the participants will begin almost immediately to think of the time when they might again sit
in a sesshin.

---

[21] Suzuki, *Zen Mind, Beginner's Mind.*

7

the sangha: community and modernity

Throughout their history Buddhists have often had difficulty defining the exact boundaries of what they mean by the Buddhist community, the sangha. There exist both narrow definitions and broad definitions. And then there are some that can only be called extraordinarily broad. But by looking at these different ways of drawing the boundaries of the sangha, we can learn something about Buddhism itself; that is because the sangha is the social expression of the dharma, one of the Three Treasures. Buddhists have always taken this matter as being very important even when they disagreed about it. Moreover, because in certain places of the world the viability of the sangha has become problematic during the twentieth century, our study of the sangha provides a good place for looking at some aspects of Buddhism in modern or modernizing societies.

The Theravada tradition has probably always had the simplest and clearest conception of what is meant by the sangha. It usually reserves this word to designate the Buddhist order of monastics. One enters the sangha by taking certain vows and by having one's hair cut off as a symbol of leaving the householding life. Often, however, this is done in stages so that a person is first tonsured and wears the white robes of an upasāka or upasīka, that is, a novice, before taking the more final step of monkhood, one that is symbolized by donning orange or saffron-colored robes and taking the full set of vows. Entry into the sangha, however, is not irrevocable; it is possible again to take off the robes and reenter the life of an ordinary householder. In fact, in some Theravada countries—especially Thailand—it is more or less assumed that all young men will be tonsured and temporarily enter the sangha before getting married;[1] some anthropologists see this as really an initiation ritual, the combination of hair cutting and vow taking in such cultures symbolizing the young man's transition from childhood to adulthood. Since the sexes are strictly segregated in the sangha, such a temporary participation in the way of life of the monks is an equivalent of the male-only societies in other cultures, which the adolescent enters for a brief, initiatory period before marriage. In that sense it is a rite of passage.[2] In such cases there would seem to be little or no intention of remaining in the sangha, although upon exit from it, it is assumed that the young person will retain his affection for it and remain a strong lay supporter of it throughout his life. In such cases there is no opprobrium attached to the departure from the sangha; even a brief sojourn within it increases a person's merit and the chance that later in life or in some later life that person will remain as a monk and make greater strides toward the eventual realization of nirvana.

Membership in the sangha is constituted in these cultures by the formal acts of an official ordination. Especially in the Theravada cultures, it is important that the rules and regulations be kept exactly since the precise performance of the requisite ritual activities determines who is inside and who is outside the sangha. In the strictest sense, even the most pious and generous of laypersons are not in the sangha, since they are still leading the householder's life, are not tonsured, and do not keep the vows of a monastic. The piety of faithful laypersons is certainly important and even necessary for the existence of the sangha. In the Theravada context, however, there is little impulse to use the word sangha broadly or to include in it those who, though still laypersons, are very devout Buddhists. One does not become a member of the sangha merely by virtue of an act of will or a spiritual devotion to the Middle Path. That is why there is a great deal of truth in saying that in such cultures you determine easily whether a person is a member of the sangha by looking to see if he or she is tonsured and wears the robe of ordination.

One other feature of the Theravada sangha is that priority of status is almost always determined by seniority, that is, the number of years one has lived as a monk. The more senior monk is one of those called a *thera,* and he usually has rank by virtue of that fact. This means there is little need for a system of determining the relative "spiritual" attainment of the monks in the sangha and no special value in engaging in a kind of spiritual one-up-manship. What is important here is not chronological age but the amount of time that has passed since entering the sangha. Although these often generally coincide so that the oldest monks are the most prestigious, it also happens that older persons who only recently were tonsured must show respect to younger ones who have been in the sangha longer.

---

[1] S. J. Tambiah, *Buddhism and the Spirit Cults in North-East Thailand* (Cambridge: Cambridge University Press, 1970), pp. 98 ff.

[2] Sam D. Gill, *Beyond "The Primitive": The Religion of Nonliterate Peoples* (Englewood Cliffs, N.J.: Prentice-Hall, 1982), pp. 77 ff.

There is, however, one other difference between monks that many say should not be overlooked. It is that between monks who live in villages and those who are hermits in the forests. Although all have taken the same vows and are officially equal in the community of monks, the forest dwellers have a spiritual status and charisma usually unavailable to the village monks, and it comes by virtue of the rigors associated with their solitary and ascetic mode of life.[3]

In any case, within the cultures of the Theravada, it can be said that the sangha can be detected by its outward, empirical signs: it is comprised of the monks who wear a special type of clothing, are able to eat by means of the alms they receive from laypersons, and live lives that fit a prescribed set of rules, the vinaya.

In the Mahayana, by contrast, the sangha is often not so neatly equivalent to the community of monks, although such a community does exist. They can be easily identified by the robes, more varied in shape and color than in the Theravada, that its members wear. The reason for this lies both in certain doctrinal developments and certain cultural ones that accompanied the Mahayana's move into East Asia. The doctrinal reason has to do with the development of the notion of the bodhisattva, one of the favored ideas within the Mahayana. Although from an early date the notion of the Buddha-to-be has been shared within all Buddhist schools, the bodhisattva—as we noted—gradually came to be regarded as a being who, in order to realize the altruistic dimension of the Middle Path, decided to postpone his or her personal nirvana in order to work for the enlightenment of other sentient beings. This is beautifully expressed in a poem by Han Yong-un (1879–1944), a Korean Buddhist monk who was also a patriot. His poem vividly presents the bodhisattva as involved in carrying others from the shore of samsara to that of nirvana.

Ferryboat and Traveler

I am the ferryboat
You are the traveler.

You tread on me with muddy feet,
I embrace you and cross over the water.
When I embrace you, deeps or shallows or fast shooting
*   rapids, I can cross over.*

When you don't come I wait from dark to dawn, in the
*   chill wind, the wet of snow and rain.*
Once over the water you go on without a glance back.

No matter, I know that sooner or later you will come.
While I wait for you, day after day I go on growing older.

---

[3] See Michael Carrithers, *The Forest Monks of Sri Lanka: An Anthropological and Historical Study* (Delhi: Oxford University Press, 1983), p. 77.

> *I am the ferryboat*
> *You are the traveler.*[4]

The line that ought to be noticed is the one that states: "When I embrace you . . . I can cross over." It crystalizes the necessity of a communal, shared salvation expressed in the bodhisattva concept.

Some Buddhists concluded that a bodhisattva so motivated would work most effectively if the existence of the glorious aspect of a bodhisattva's being were kept under covers, that is, *hidden* from the eyes of most mortals. This led to the notion of the bodhisattva appearing incognito, often even in human bodily forms or in conditions of dress far different from what most would consider "appropriate" for such a being. That is, the purposes of such a being would often be best served if its heart were that of a bodhisattva but its exterior appearance and demeanor were something else altogether. Clearly for a bodhisattva always to wear a monk's robes or have a halo over its head could impede the altruistic purpose.

This fit certain cultural needs of the East Asian peoples. It also made the acceptance of Buddhism much more easy than it otherwise would have been, especially in China. It meant, for instance, that ancient or even contemporary "sages" honored by Taoists and Confucianists could come to be regarded by the Chinese as Buddhist bodhisattvas who lived in China without revealing their nature as figures in the Buddhist panoply of exalted beings. For the Japanese, it meant that many of the Shinto *kami* that had been respected from archaic times could be seen as having been manifestations of Buddhas and bodhisattvas even long before the explicit knowledge of Śākyamuni's teachings arrived in Japan. Naturally this meant that Buddhism could be assimilated to existing religious frameworks much more easily than if it had come into these cultures with the assumption that existing gods had to be jettisoned and existing teachings had to be displaced by what was new.

On the other hand, of course, it meant that in the fullest sense, the community of Buddhists was not limited to those who explicitly espoused Śākyamuni's Middle Way; it included many who taught wisely or acted humanely, even though they seemed to have no *overt* connection whatsoever with the Middle Way as professed within the teachings that came from India. In fact, within East Asia the notion of the bodhisattva was extremely powerful; ideally this figure would not rest in nirvana until *all sentient beings* were saved and brought with him into final nirvana. But the reference to "all sentient beings" is a very wide one indeed; it articulates the notion of universal salvation. To most of the thinkers of the Mahayana, this meant that in its widest sense, the sangha included all beings, whether they are currently aware that they possess Buddha-nature or not. Universalism was the natural and logical position to maintain.

---

[4] Trans. by Sammy E. Solberg in *The Silence of Love: Twentieth-Century Korean Poetry*, ed. by Peter H. Lee (Honolulu: The University of Hawaii Press, 1980), p. 15.

This is shown by one interesting historical episode. A relatively early Chinese Buddhist scholar named Tao-sheng (ca. 360–420 C.E.) had concluded that the very logic of the Mahayana made it necessary to hold that all beings would eventually reach Buddha-hood. His problem was that among the Sanskrit texts translated into Chinese by that point in history, there was none that taught this in exactly so many words. Moreover, in some Indian texts there were references to the *icchantika*, a category of beings who were so self-absorbed that they seemed to be beyond the pale of even an eventual salvation. In spite of this, however, Tao-sheng came to the bold conclusion that even icchantikas would eventually achieve Buddha-hood. Although he himself risked censure from the order of monks in defending this version of universal salvation, Tao-sheng was eventually vindicated when later the full translation of the *Mahāparinirvāna-sūtra* stated his own position explicitly.[5] In the final analysis, this aspect of things fit not only the logic of the doctrine of the Mahayana but also the cultural and intellectual proclivities of the Chinese. The same was true for the Koreans and Japanese.

One other development in the Mahayana conceptions of the Buddhist community deserves attention. It too arises, at least in part, from the familiar portrait of the bodhisattva as one working for the enlightenment of all sentient beings. In some texts, perhaps originally as a figure of speech, it was said that they were willing to wait and work until "the last blade of grass" had realized its Buddha-hood. This figure of speech raised an interesting question: Were trees and plants included too in the category of those with Buddha-hood? It was a question that brought forth a good deal of debate among the Chinese and the Japanese.

To most Buddhists, it had always seemed obvious that animals had some form of Buddha-nature. At least through progression up the scale of beings, such creatures might eventually be reborn as human beings and then as practitioners of the Middle Path might be able to attain their enlightenment at long last. That potential for Buddha-hood was often pictorially represented. The Chinese were fond of picturing even ferocious tigers as lying down peacefully with bodhisattvas and wise men—a tribute both to the sages' ability to pacify wild beings and to the innate Buddha-nature even in tigers and the like. The Japanese, who knew tigers only through pictures, tended to see Buddha-nature in more benign forms of animal life. As noticed in their art and poetry, they saw it in frogs that seemed to them to meditate even as they sit in and in horses that often appeared to show kindness and gentleness in spite of their size and power.

The Buddha-hood of plants and trees, however, was a more difficult position to maintain. The important question was whether or not plants were to be included in the category of sentient beings. The Buddhist philosophers of medieval China and medieval Japan found it an interesting question and one that they debated back and forth for centuries. The direction of these discussions led more and more toward the acceptance of vegetable life as included in the chain of beings with Bud-

---

[5] Kenneth K. S. Ch'en, *Buddhism in China: A Historical Survey* (Princeton, N.J.: Princeton University Press, 1964), pp. 113–116.

dha-nature. In Japan, the discussions were especially lively, and in the year 963 a public debate on the topic had imperial sponsorship in the capital city and was attended by many interested monks and laypersons. One Buddhist philosopher who advocated the positive side of the argument was the monk Ryōgen (912-985). His arguments are interesting. He took note of the fact that the really adept Buddhist practitioner learns to sit in quiet, his body almost unmoving in meditation. Even Śākyamuni sat in such a way when he reached enlightenment. Ryōgen stated that that is precisely what a tree or plant does when it sits rooted firmly in one place. He claimed that the seeds out of which the tree grows are really the seeds of enlightenment, that in practicing like a yogi in one spot, the plant is undergoing the necessary disciplines, that in flowering it is putting forth the fruit of its enlightenment, and that in passing away without outcry or protest it is entering into its own parinirvāna.[6] The interesting thing in this is that what had begun as a discussion of the "possibility" that plants and trees had a potential for Buddha-hood became— especially, perhaps, because the Japanese have traditionally had such a love for trees and plants—a case for the *certainty* of their enlightenment. They became, in fact, things honored for their attainment of Buddha-hood as they are; it became unnecessary to think of them as going through later rebirths in order to enter nirvana at some future date. Plants and trees in their tranquil stillness became even models for man to follow.

The notion of drawing an exact line where the sangha begins and where it ends became, obviously, very problematic for those in the Mahayana tradition— especially if they were East Asians with a very strong desire to think in terms of the eventual salvation of all beings. Sometimes this universalism had a strong effect on practical morality as, for instance, when many Chinese concluded that it was a form of "murder" to eat animal flesh. For many of them, being Buddhist implied being vegetarian. And if they could not be vegetarian all the time, they tried to be such on certain special days. In China the practice of releasing caged birds and placing caught fish back into their natural waters became much revered forms of Buddhist practice. Buddhist thinkers praised such deeds and even emperors performed them.[7] Sometimes, however, universalism seems to have had the opposite effect— such as, for instance, when Japanese Buddhists, after having tried to be somewhat vegetarian, historically moved back again to eating meat. This change took place quite rapidly after their renewed contact in the nineteenth century with meat-eating Westerners, but a conceptual basis had been laid by pushing the boundaries of Buddha-hood to all beings, including plants. After all, when even vegetation has Buddha-nature, that leaves nothing for man to eat. They concluded that, with proper reverence and with thanks to the creatures whose lives were taken to be food, the eating of meat was not, after all, so much a violation of Buddhist morality.

---

[6] William R. LaFleur, "Saigyō and the Buddhist Value of Nature," *History of Religions,* Vol. 13, nos. 2, 3(Nov. 1973 and Feb. 1974), pp. 93-128 and 227-248.

[7] Chün-fang Yu, *The Renewal of Buddhism in China: Chu-hung and the Late Ming Synthesis* (New York: Columbia University Press, 1981), pp. 66-87.

LAMA

There are, of course, many different types of relationship between the Buddhist sangha and the societies in which that sangha finds itself. These differences make for much of the variety among Buddhist cultures. But perhaps one of the most interesting of these is the one that developed over the centuries in Tibet. Among Westerners it has been the subject of a good deal of curiosity—perhaps because Tibet as a whole has been a source of fascination and fantasy in the West for many years. It has also been the subject of a good deal of misunderstanding, and, therefore, it is important that we describe the traditional Tibetan sangha as accurately as we can.

Usually in the past Tibet was imagined by Westerners to be one of the most strange and unapproachable societies on earth. To some it was romantically envisioned as some kind of Shangri-la behind the mountains of central Asia, a land that was an idyllic hideaway. Others saw it as a place where people remained intensely spiritual, still untainted by the doubts, skepticisms, and pragmatic worldliness of modern life. At the other extreme there were people who depicted Tibet as a land of forbidding climate and an entire population under the sway of a corrupt Buddhist clergy that perpetuated silly superstitions and pandered to the populace with magic tricks. These people complained about the dust and dirt they found in Tibet; they also felt revulsion when seeing the sex and the skulls that figure largely in the Buddhist tantric art of that culture. To them Tibet was hopelessly sunken in either a primitive or, at most, a medieval cultural frame, unable to appreciate the values of modern science and modern life as these had come to be articulated in the West. The thing to notice about this is that in almost all books written by Westerners during the early twentieth century there was little place for balanced, accurate views; Tibet either was romanticized beyond belief or portrayed as a society that was dirty, debased, and despicably archaic.

In those books Buddhism in traditional Tibet was almost always referred to simply with one word. That word was "lamaism," an English word made by adding the suffix "ism" to *blama,* the Tibetan word (pronounced lama) used to translate the Indian word and concept for a personal religious teacher, that is, a guru. The word "lamaism" deserves to be looked at carefully. Sometimes the suffix "ism" can have a neutral implication, but often it is added to describe something thought to be excessive or abnormal. At least when you read the older type of book about Tibet, you can very quickly notice that its use was often pejorative; through it the writer was expressing the view that the numbers, presence, and influence of Buddhist religious teachers in Tibet was excessive, simply too much to make for anything like a healthy society. You can go on to read in those books the portrayal of the Tibetan monks as dirty, corrupt, eager only for power, and purveyors of the grossest kinds of superstition. No doubt some of this depiction in negative terms was due to the fact that many accounts were written by Christian missionaries who were eager to show that Tibet needed Christianity and the benefits of Western culture. But even persons otherwise sympathetic to Buddhism often accepted the com-

Lama Rig-'dzin

mon account of Tibet's Buddhism as one that had departed very far from the early norms and values of Śākyamuni; for instance, during his otherwise often perceptive tour of Asia during the 1920s, an American philosopher, James B. Pratt, decided he would not bother going to Tibet since, in his words its Buddhism was "so mixed with non-Buddhist elements that I hesitate to call it Buddhism at all."[8] Clearly, then, the understanding of the Buddhism traditionally practiced in the Land of Snows is one that is gotten only with considerable difficulty.

We have suggested that one place we may begin is with the term "lamaism."

---

[8] James Bissett Pratt, *The Pilgrimage of Buddhism and a Buddhist Pilgrimage* (New York: Macmillan, 1928), p. viii.

Even though it was often used disparagingly in the past and does not adequately express the complexity of Buddhism in Tibet, many scholars today are quite willing to see in it an element of truth. That is, it points up the fact that any attempt to understand the sangha of Tibet must recognize the crucial role there of the lama or guru in traditional religious life. But the term lama may not be applied indiscriminately to everyone in Tibet who became a Buddhist monk, as, for instance, our dictionaries often define the term. It should be reserved and used only for those who serve as personal spiritual teacher or master. It refers to the qualified master or teacher who is fit to transmit his teachings to a student who has come to the point of being qualified to receive them. And in this the Tibetans are not mavericks; they differ from Buddhists of other lands only in the *degree* to which they place emphasis upon the master. David L. Snellgrove rightly notes:

> When the Tibetans insist, as they certainly do, that without a religious teacher (lama) to guide one, one can make no progress in the religious life, they are not pronouncing a teaching which is peculiarly Tibetan, but one which is quite generally Buddhist.[9]

For instance in Ch'an or Zen Buddhism, the emphasis upon direct transmission from teacher to student also assumes great importance. Also in the Japanese form of esoteric Buddhism derived from Kūkai (774–835), which itself has tantric elements ultimately derived from India,[10] the intimacy of the master-disciple relationship is crucial for an adequate transmission of the dharma.

In the Tibetan Buddhist tradition, this transmission is one in which the recipient must prove his or her readiness to receive the teaching. That is, some kind of examination is required; the lama must put his potential disciple to the test. But the exact nature of that examination may vary widely, and here that considerable variety within the Tibetan sangha can be noted. For instance, in the ancient Nyingma-pa school that honors the Indian Padmasambhava and in the Kagyü-pa school that derived from the ascetic poet Milarepa (1040–1123), there is a great deal of emphasis upon yogic and meditation practices through which the aspirant not only concretely learns the meaning of the dharma but also attains certain powers that some might think of as extraordinary and even supernatural. To that extent, the testing of the disciple by the master is almost a classic case of a rite of initiation. The most important thing, however, is the degree of faith that the disciple demonstrates in his teacher—in spite of the sometimes seemingly cruel ordeals prescribed by the latter. In the eyes of his disciple, the position of the lama must be even higher than that of the Buddhas, and even what appear to be imposed suf-

---

[9] David L. Snellgrove, "Tibetan Buddhism Today," in Heinrich Dumoulin, ed., *Buddhism in the Modern World* (New York: Macmillan, 1976), p. 279.

[10] See Yoshito S. Hakeda, *Kūkai: Major Works* (New York and London: Columbia University Press, 1972), and Minoru Kiyota, *Shingon Buddhism: Theory and Practice* (Los Angeles and Tokyo: Buddhist Books International, 1978), pp. 5–25.

ferings are to be greeted and accepted as kindnesses. All of this is to release the aspirant from his own attachment to the fiction of his own atman or self—although it is easy to see why outside observers, especially those from the West, interpreted all this as mere cruelty and had no inkling concerning the inner intention.

Some historians of religion have pointed out that this willingness on the part of many Tibetan Buddhists to push to the outer limits of physical and mental endurance fits the historic development of the tantric form of Buddhism but also shows a remarkable affinity to the ancient pattern of shamanism that was such an important part of the spiritual life of many Siberian, Mongolian, and Tibetan people. For in the archaic shamanism of these cultures, a high value had always been placed on the success with which an initiate goes through a ritual death and rebirth ritual. He becomes one with an inner knowledge of the passage through death, going even to the extent of envisioning the dismemberment of his own flesh and of "seeing" his own skeleton. Here is where Buddhism incorporated within itself earlier religious patterns. According to Mircea Eliade, in Tibet:

> this type of meditation belongs to an archaic, pre-Buddhist stratum of spirituality, which was based . . . on the ideology of hunting peoples (the sacredness of bones) and whose object was to "withdraw" the soul from the practitioner's own body for a mystical journey—that is, to achieve ecstasy.[11]

This helps to explain why Tibetan monks will often use human bones and skulls as part of their rituals. It also suggests the reason for the personal mystique many of them have gained as men in whom the fear of death is no longer present. It very well may have a basis in the shamanism that was and remains such an important aspect of the cultural areas of Asia, but this shamanism has been given new meaning and import by the traditions of Buddhism, according to which there is the need to confront the inescapable fact of one's own impermanence (anitya) and personally recapitulate Śākyamuni's own experience of seeing a corpse. In the Tibetan cultural region, the "meditation on the foul" and the confrontation with one's own impermanence become highly charged and highly personalized. In the process of this, the attachment to an inadequate version of one's self, the ego-based one, falls away. In some sense, at least psychologically and spiritually, a new person is said to be born.

In view of this, it is not too difficult to see how earlier Westerners jumped to one or the other extreme in their account of Tibet's sangha, seeing it either as a group of monks capable of uncommon, almost superhuman levels of spiritual athleticism or as a society of charlatans who could not possibly be capable of the feats attributed to them. Both the romanticizers and the denigrators of Tibetan lamas tended to exaggerate the facts, but beneath those exaggerations was an actual pattern of religious behavior—especially that of asceticism—that was quite different from what Westerners knew in their own cultures.

---

[11] Mircea Eliade, *Shamanism: Archaic Techniques of Ecstasy* (Princeton, N.J.: Princeton University Press, 1964), p. 435.

Later in Tibet's history the test of a student by his teacher took on another dimension: his mastery of learning, the written canon of scriptures, and examination in the methods of formal debate. This became especially important in the Gelug-pa, a school founded by the great scholar-master Tsong-kha-pa (1357–1419). The Gelug-pa began as a reform movement in the Tibetan sangha and gradually gained wide and enthusiastic support within Tibet. It is especially the monasteries of this order that have impressed Westerners, either as wonderful treasures of human culture or as institutions too archaic to subsist in the modern world. Earlier in our century some of these monasteries were the largest in the world and existed at a time when as much as a third of Tibet's male population was comprised of Buddhist monks.

These monasteries were really the universities of Tibet and Central Asia; they were established on the pattern of the great ones such as Nālandā in India. In them not only classical Buddhist philosophy was taught but also what some would call the more secular arts and sciences: medicine, mathematics, literature, astronomy, astrology, and the various traditions of the visual and plastic arts. R. A. Stein continues:

> From monasteries lastly, as in medieval Europe, came the book, as manuscript of xylographic block-print, edition and impression.[12]

The comparison with medieval Europe is apt—and a reason for much of the conflict in contemporary opinion about Tibet. To some this added to its attractiveness; here in the Tibetan Himalayas they could locate places that remained full and intact embodiments of a medieval culture, somehow wonderfully preserved and undisturbed right down to the middle of the twentieth century. Others regarded that medieval quality as the bane of existence there since, in their judgment at least, a society that is medieval is also one that incorporates feudalism, serfs forced to struggle to exist on soil that was difficult to farm, and social institutions in which conflict was rife.[13] And, of course, among those who deplored this side of Tibetan life and said it should continue no longer have been Marxists and Maoists; this criticism was the stated reason for the Chinese incorporation of Tibet into China's own territory in the 1950s.

As a venue for the more scholarly side of Tibetan Buddhism, however, the Gelug-pa order deserves attention. It was also the school that brought forth one of Tibet's best known traditions, that of the Dalai Lama, and it is here that we can get somewhat closer to defining the uniqueness of Tibet's sangha. We noted earlier that having spiritual progress depend upon transmission from a revered teacher—whom the Tibetans call a lama—is, in fact, a practice shared fairly widely within Buddhist cultures, even though other cultures do not use the term lama as such. But the

---

[12] Stein, *Tibetan Civilization* (Stanford: Stanford U. Press, 1972), p. 156.

[13] Melvyn C. Goldstein, "The Circulation of Estates in Tibet: Reincarnation, Land, and Politics," *Journal of Asian Studies,* Vol. 32, no. 3 (May 1973), 445–455.

Tibetans added something new. With the development of their large Buddhist monasteries and the need to have men worthy of great reverence as abbots or heads of those communities, the monks began to recognize these abbots as reincarnations of recently deceased great teachers. This practice goes back at least as far as the twelfth century. The interesting thing about this is not that a great teacher could be thought of as a new incarnation of earlier ones since that belief is fairly common among Buddhists even if also quite generalized in conception. But the Tibetan sangha began to recognize them as *specific* reincarnations and saw the discovery of such a person as the basis for the elevation of him to the primacy within a particular monastery. In other words, upon the death of an abbot-master the sangha of that monastery took steps to find the child in whom their deceased leader was now again reincarnated. Then as still a child, this reincarnated one would be brought to the monastery, highly revered by all there, and trained in the duties of the abbotship. The curious feature of this is that, although the new abbot is technically the "successor" of the former one, he is in fact considered to be the *same* person reincarnated.

Because there were multiple monasteries in Tibet, there were also multiple reincarnation traditions. That of the Dalai Lama began as one of these; it originated within the Gelug-pa school. Although at the time the term "Dalai" was actually not yet part of the official title, the person now thought to have been the first Dalai Lama (1391-1474) is regarded as the fifty-first reincarnation of the bodhisattva Avalokiteśvara. Although as a reformist movement the Gelug-pa order for some time had not engaged in political affairs, in the sixteenth century there developed a close relationship between the Drepung monastery of that school and Mongolians with great political power. It was at that time that the Mongolians, who then were converting to Tibetan Buddhism, bestowed the term "Dalai," which means "ocean" in Mongolian, on the abbot of Drepung monastery. "Dalai" was not a Tibetan word, and even today, although known and used by Westerners, it is not one of the terms the Tibetans themselves use to refer to their most revered lama. Then in 1642 certain Mongolians assumed political power in Tibet and established the fifth Dalai Lama in the capital of Lhasa as the religious ruler of the country.[14] Since Avalokiteśvara is the patron bodhisattva of Tibet, it was natural for the institution of the Dalai Lama, one in which this figure is assumed to be repeatedly reincarnated, to receive immense prestige in Tibet. This prestige eventually encompassed not only spiritual but also temporal matters. Until at least 1959 the incumbent of this position was the virtual ruler of Tibet; his Lhasa residence was in the Potala, a building of monumental proportions that is one of the architectural wonders of the world. And since the Dalai Lama has always been a monk and part of the sangha, there is a sense in which during these centuries Tibet has been a land ruled both spiritually and politically by its Buddhist sangha. It is for this reason that early Western travelers to Tibet often called it a theocracy.

---

[14] Stein, *Tibetan Civilization*, p. 139.

The uniqueness of this situation deserves further attention. One of its interesting features is the manner in which, upon the death of one Dalai Lama, his successor or reincarnation is located. The potential problem facing the authorities is immense: how to find the *one* child in all of Tibet in whom the deceased has chosen to reincarnate himself. The process is complex, and divination plays a large part in it; also it usually requires at least a couple of years to complete. Traditional doctrine maintains that a period of forty-nine days separates the date of the one lama's death and his reappearance through birth.[15] Those charged with finding the exact child in which the deceased has reincarnated will search for clues, for instance, in things said by the last Dalai Lama before he expired or in mysterious shifts in the direction faced by his corpse soon after he died. There is also a sacred lake in Tibet where those qualified have sometimes seen visions that give hints concerning the rebirth. After that, specially qualified search parties are dispatched to the general area of expectation. First they locate male children whose birthdate corresponds to the deathdate plus forty-nine days. Then they proceed to test all possible candidates. They do this especially by showing them personal possessions of the deceased lama—spectacles, pencils, rosaries, and the like—interspersed among an array of many items that did not belong to him. The true candidate, it is assumed, will quite easily identify those that belonged to himself in his earlier incarnation, since it is basically a matter of recognition of things that were once his own. Also the ability to remember one's own past is traditionally considered a quality of such highly achieved lamas, especially one deemed to be a bodhisattva. Then a physical examination follows; bodily marks confirm the choice and include the presence of things such as eyebrows that curve up at the ends, large ears, and a conch-shell impression on one palm.[16] When the discovery has been confirmed, the child lama will be taken into the sangha and his immediate family will be ennobled and become part of the highest stratum of Tibetan society.[17]

This does not mean, however, that the life of the Dalai Lama has always been easy. Because it is the center not only of spiritual but also of political power in Tibet, it has often been a position that others, including monks in quest of personal power, have sought to manipulate. Historically, a surprisingly large percentage of Dalai Lamas have died young or in mysterious circumstances.[18] Then in 1959 Tibet's situation changed drastically. Due to the fact that the Chinese had by that point assumed political control over most of Tibet's territory, the fourteenth Dalai Lama, who was born in 1935, was forced to flee Tibet and take up residence in India. He was followed by approximately 100,000 of his fellow countrymen who

---

[15] See *The Tibetan Book of the Dead,* trans. by Francesca Fremantle and Chögyam Trungpa (Boulder, Colo., and London: Shambala, 1975).

[16] Dalai Lama XIVth, *My Land and My People* (New York: McGraw-Hill, 1962), pp. 20–25.

[17] Goldstein, "The Circulation of Estates," p. 449.

[18] Robert A. Paul, *The Tibetan Symbolic World: Psychoanalytic Explorations* (Chicago and London: University of Chicago Press, 1982), pp. 297–298.

settled in India, Europe, and America. The story of the exiled Tibetans' fierce but militarily unsuccessful struggle to recapture their own land has been told by many observers;[19] it confirms David L. Snellgrove's observation about:

> the essential toughness of Tibetan religion, which all too often has been portrayed by modern Tibetophiles as though it were a kind of self-resigning meekness in suffering. Tibetan monks, as well as laymen, have always been fighters, especially when their religion is threatened.[20]

Certainly one of the results of the expatriation on the part of many Tibetans as well as most of their principal lamas has been the opportunity for Westerners to inspect Tibetan Buddhism more closely than before—even though, of course, these studies could not be carried on in their original setting. Scholarly study has been largely of two types: one has involved mastery of the difficult written language and work translating the extensive Buddhist canon of texts, whereas the other has been comprised of field studies by trained anthropologists who, through observations and interviews, have described many of the details and structures of traditional Tibetan religious life. Another unforeseen result of the forced exile of much of the community of lamas has been their accessibility to Westerners who themselves have been eager to study with them as their own spiritual masters. This has taken place both in India where many lamas now live and also in communities in Europe and America where certain lamas have resettled and begun to teach.

The institution of the Dalai Lama is not only a unique institution within the Buddhist sangha but in the Buddhist world is the closest thing to the Christian institution of the papacy. There are, of course, great differences, not only in the manner of transmission and the teachings behind it but also in the extent of actual spiritual authority; that of the Dalai Lama extends to relatively few of the world's Buddhists. Nevertheless the Dalai Lama, probably particularly in the eyes of many Westerners, commands unusual respect as a spokesman for Buddhism in the modern world. The comparison with the papacy is evident in the fact that now in English it has become proper to refer to him as "His Holiness." Since leaving Tibet, the fourteenth Dalai Lama has traveled to various countries of Asia and also to the West. During his visits to America, he has received not only the reverence of people here who honor him as their spiritual leader but also considerable attention from the public press.

During the summer of 1976, I was granted a private interview with him at his palace in Dharamsala in northwestern India. When I arrived at the community of Tibetan refugees who have resettled in that area, I was told that, since His Holiness was engaged in a spiritual retreat, any chance of a meeting was highly unlikely. But I had time to wait and the need to do so gave me an opportunity to learn what I

---

[19] See, for example, John F. Avedon, *In Exile from the Land of Snow* (New York: Knopf, 1984).
[20] Snellgrove, "Tibetan Buddhism Today," p. 286.

could from the intensely devout Buddhists whose communities lie high up on the sides of the mountains there—a topographical placement probably as much like that of their native Tibet as they can find in India. I appreciated the chance to see the collection of sutras in the Library of Tibetan Archives there on the mountain and the procession of pious laypeople who daily circumambulated the library many times over, the way in which they approximate the manner in which the devout used to circumambulate the Potala in Lhasa. The days passed quickly. Then just as the monsoon rains were arriving and it became important for me to make my departure, I learned that I would be given an hour with His Holiness. In the rain I literally scrambled up the mountainside to the place where his modest palace is located.

Among the things that stand out in my memory of that hour is the question he early on posed to me. Having learned that I had studied Japanese Buddhism, he asked me how the interests of the Japanese Buddhists differed from those of the Tibetans. The only thing I could mention was the fascination of the medieval Japanese with the question whether or not plants and trees had Buddha-nature, since I suspected this problem had never been a great one among the Tibetans. In that I guessed correctly; the Dalai Lama was indeed curious about this and wanted to know the details of the discussions and debates held by the Japanese. Together we noted that the differing topography and ecology of Tibet and Japan—the substratum of culture—probably prompted these differing historic concerns among the two peoples. In all of this I was much impressed with his deep intellectual curiosity, especially concerning the variety of teaching and practices within the Buddhist world. This confirmed an impression I had received in Japan some years earlier when I had seen him interviewed on television in Tokyo by a panel of Japanese scholars of Buddhism.

I asked him about the long-range significance of the exile of himself and many of his fellow Buddhists from Tibet. In his response he showed that his concern was not limited to his fellow Tibetans alone, even though their situation was the one felt most keenly and painfully. He noted that in our century many smaller cultures, long able to retain a distinct religious and cultural life in their own settings, have suddenly been inundated by the cultures and also by the ideologies of larger ones. Sometimes these smaller peoples seem to be completely swallowed up in these larger, more powerful and aggressive cultures—whether these be of the East or of the West. Tibet is an instance of this unfortunate pattern that has plagued so much of our era. This kind of thing has had an unfortunate effect on our world as a whole, in terms of its diversity and overall richness; it has made it culturally more homogeneous. His wish, in addition to that of returning to Tibet, is that what has happened to Tibet might still signal the need for worldwide attention to this distressing process and the way in which it is making our world religiously and culturally poorer than it once was. Concerning what will happen in Tibet, he refrained from speculation, merely noting that, although things often look bleak for the existence of the Buddhist sangha there, the people of Tibet have in the past tended to be remarkably tenacious in their faith. The future may, he said, take twists and turns we today cannot imagine and anticipate.

MONKS ABLAZE

At least one thing about the Buddhist sangha in the twentieth century seems quite certain: more than ever before in its history it has been forced to reevaluate and sometimes even alter its traditional modes of existence in various societies. Much of the origin of this problem lay in earlier centuries, especially for nations such as Sri Lanka, Burma, Cambodia, Laos, and Vietnam, which for many years had been forced to be colonies of European powers. Thailand was the only Theravada country that retained its independence. The years of colonization for the Buddhist nations were also years during which missionaries from Europe and America tried to convert people from Buddhism to Christianity. During those years—centuries in some cases—the Buddhist sangha declined considerably both in terms of its role in society and its prestige. At the same time, it waited for the end of the colonial era and the departure of the missionaries. It seldom entered into real conflict with the Christians, although most Theravada Buddhists remained convinced that their own form of religious philosophy was much more rational and even scientific than that of Christianity; many Buddhists were happy to state and underscore this point. For instance, in Sri Lanka, then known as Ceylon, during the nineteenth century even an American, Henry S. Olcott, was a participant in a revival of Buddhism there. Olcott had studied Buddhism quite extensively and was convinced of its superiority. In Sri Lanka during the 1880s, he publicly debated with representatives of Christianity, promoted Buddhist education at a time when it was weak, and helped the Buddhists there to gain certain freedoms for the practice of their religion. Although the contribution of one American to the revival of Buddhism was, of course, much less than that of the many Asians most directly involved, Olcott's importance lay in the fact that he was an educated Westerner who claimed to have found in Theravada Buddhism a religious philosophy totally amenable to the critical and scientific mind of modern man. Grateful for his services, the Buddhists of Sri Lanka still annually observe a holiday known as Henry S. Olcott Day.

But even with the end of colonialism the severe problems facing the sangha did not go away. That is primarily because rival economic and political systems that had their origins in the West have vied with one another through much of the twentieth century and one of their major venues has been in Asia. One nation that was very much caught up in this rivalry, tragically so, was Vietnam. For many people, especially in America, the history of Vietnam in the twentieth century is one they would rather forget. But during America's protracted political and military involvement in Vietnam, there were numberless mistakes of judgment made by the Americans, and many of these were undoubtedly due, at least in part, to the fact that Westerners so tragically misunderstood the thinking and concerns of the Buddhist sangha in that country.

This misunderstanding clearly came to the surface in 1963. At that point the French, who had been waging a struggle against insurgents in South Vietnam, had largely given up that struggle as a losing one; in their stead, the American government was beginning to pour aid of various kinds into Vietnam to strengthen the Saigon government that was comprised almost entirely of Catholics. Vietnam had for a long time been colonized and Christianized by the French, and many Catholics were in high positions. To many Westerners, especially if they knew the country only superficially, Vietnam seemed locked in a struggle between Marxists on the one hand and on the other capitalists who were most often also Christians. Buddhism seemed a religion only of Vietnam's past, a now thin Mahayana veneer laid over folk religious practices. To them Buddhism seemed to have little hold on the minds of the people, especially in Saigon (now Ho Chi Mihn City), at that time the capital of the south. In addition, educated Westerners who had read some things about the sociology of the world's religions had often been told in those books that Buddhism is the faith of a community of tonsured monks who were intent on "world rejection" and the pursuit only of their own private nirvanas. This, they assumed, meant that the sangha had no interest or stake in what was happening in society. That sangha could be expected to carry on in its traditionally benign fashion while others in society, world-affirming Marxists and Catholics, would carry on their fight for the control of South Vietnam. This was a widely held assumption in the West.

This explains why the events of 1963 came as such a surprise and such a shock. In May a crowd of Buddhist monks and laymen gathered in the city of Hue to protest the actions of the Catholic archbishop who recently had forbidden Buddhists to carry the Buddhist flag when celebrating the traditional birthday of Śākyamuni. They were fired on and nine were killed. Then on June 11 something very unexpected happened. According to eyewitness reports an automobile filled with monks arrived at the busy intersection of Le Van Duyet and Phan Dinh Phung streets in Saigon. The monks got out and other monks and nuns who were already there formed a circle around one of their number, a seventy-three-year-old monk named Thich Quang Duc, who seated himself on the asphalt. He took the cross-legged lotus posture and the Buddhists around him began to chant sutras. Gasoline was poured over his body until he was thoroughly soaked with it. Then the aged monk very calmly struck a match and ignited himself.

> Instantly he was engulfed in a whoosh of flame. . . . The smoke rose and, as the fierce flames brightened, Quang Duc's face, his shaven skull, and his robes grizzled, then blackened. Amidst the devouring flames his body remained fixed in meditation.[21]

David Halberstam, a correspondent for *The New York Times*, had just arrived on the scene and saw this monk incinerating himself. He wrote:

> As he burned he never moved a muscle, never uttered a sound, his outward composure in sharp contrast to the wailing people around him. I had never felt such conflicting emotions.[22]

---

[21] Jerrold Schecter, *The New Face of Buddha: Buddhism and Political Power in Southeast Asia* (Tokyo: Weatherhill, 1967), p. 166.

[22] David Halberstam, *The Making of a Quagmire* (New York: Random House, 1964), p. 211.

Halberstam also noted that he, like many other Westerners, up to this point had simply never taken the Buddhist majority of Vietnam seriously:

> To us the Buddhist monks were strange little men in orange robes—distant, faceless, little Asians. Like Americans in Vietnam, we were concerned with the war, . . . knew little about Vietnamese Buddhism and had never been in a pagoda.[23]

This was only the first of a series of such meditative self-immolations on the part of monks and nuns of Vietnam. Most were explicitly linked to the compassion felt by these Buddhists for their countrymen after years of suffering caused by war—at that time a war intensified by outside arms and armies from two different political systems. The analysis of the significance of the events of 1963 and their aftermath continued for years. Among the many lessons said to have been learned was the one that Westerners' willful ignorance of other religious systems can be a major contributor to international tragedy. This would seem to be especially so when it is combined with a disdain for religions considered to be unconcerned with modern political and social events.

What happened in Vietnam actually can provide an excellent context for study of the sangha's complex act of balancing tradition and modernity. First, however, it should be noted that the Buddhism of twentieth century Vietnam is unique in that it is the only country in Asia where both Mahayana and Theravada forms of Buddhism have coexisted in modern times. The latter came from India and was practiced by the Khmer people in the Mekong Delta, whereas the peoples farther north had learned their Buddhism from the Chinese. This had been of the Mahayana type—mostly Thien, a form of the Ch'an or Zen school, and Tinh-do or the Pure Land school. Whereas Thien emphasized the sangha of celibate monks, the Tinh-do form—as in China and Japan—traditionally placed a high value on the practice of laypersons.[24] The exact date of Buddhism's beginnings in Vietnam cannot be determined, but by the ninth century it was the Chinese forms that were most powerful there. These traditions remained strong for a thousand years but then in the nineteenth century seemed to begin to weaken, especially as Westernization and the work of Catholic missionaries intensified.

In spite of this, however, in the twentieth century, Vietnamese Buddhism experienced a movement of reform and revitalization. Study groups were organized and Western scholars' attention to the teachings of early Buddhism gave new prestige to the smaller Theravada tradition in Vietnam, for which new monasteries were now established in the south.[25] Although some members of the sangha showed increasing interest in the relationship between Buddhism and society, the twentieth-

---

[23] Halberstam, *Quagmire,* p. 196.

[24] Heinz Bechert and Vu Duy-Tu, "Buddhism in Vietnam," in Heinrich Dumoulin, ed., *Buddhism in the Modern World* (New York: Macmillan, 1976), p. 189.

[25] Heinz Bechert and Vu Duy-Tu, "Buddhism in Vietnam," p. 190.

century revival had few political overtones until the 1960s. Then it was undoubt-edly the Saigon government's blatant disregard of the Buddhists' concern for the nation's suffering that led to the events of 1963 and beyond.

It was, however, not from the Theravada but from the Mahayana tradition that precedents for self-immolation derived. In fact, in the Theravada anything that would appear to be suicide was forbidden by the sangha's own rules:

> [Śākyamuni] the Blessed One . . . laid down this precept: "Priests, let no one destroy himself, and whosoever would destroy himself, let him be dealt with according to law."[26]

Of course, both traditions stress the fact of impermanence and the following poem by an eleventh-century Vietnamese monk named Van Hanh, though employing fire as a metaphor for human life generally, today sounds like something that almost anticipated the events of 1963:

Last Words to Disciples

A flash—the body is, then is no more.
All plants in springtime thrive, in autumn fade.
Let fortune wheel, dread not its rise and fall—
A dewdrop poised atop a leaf of grass.[27]

The known precedents for the firey deaths of Thich Quang Duc and others, how-ever, all come from the Mahayana tradition, where there is no such proscription against suicide for a worthy cause. For instance, the Lotus Sutra, a text that is im-portant in the Mahayana and to the Buddhists of China, describes the pious act of Bodhisattva Medicine King, someone who in a former life had vowed to heal the diseases of all beings. At the crucial point in the text he states that, although he had made many offerings, he had never offered his own body. Then the narrative continues:

> Straightway then he applied to his body various scents . . . and he also drank the fragrant oils of campaka-flowers. [Then] . . . he wrapped his body in a garment adorned with divine jewels, annointed himself with fragrant oils, with the force of supernatural penetration took a vow, and then burnt his body. The glow gave light all around to the world-spheres equal in number to the sands of eighty millions of Ganges rivers. Within them the Buddhas all at once praised him . . .[28]

---

[26] *Milindapanha,* in Warren, *Buddhism in Translations,* p. 437.
[27] In *The Heritage of Vietnamese Poetry,* ed. and trans. by Huynh Sanh Thong (New Haven, Conn., and London: Yale University Press, 1979), p. 18.
[28] Leon Hurvitz, trans., *Scripture of the Lotus Blossom of the Fine Dharma* (New York: Columbia University Press, 1976), pp. 294-295.

This text originated in India, and there is no indication from other sources that any Indian Buddhist ever performed this type of offering. But when the Mahayana reached China, there were people who took its message literally. Their reasons were multiple.

Often they immolated themselves as acts of personal piety. As such these were even more extreme examples of the kind of thing the Confucian Han Yü severely criticized in China when, as we have seen, in his own day some Buddhists seemed willing to cut off their fingers to demonstrate their devotion. But there are also recorded instances of immolation or other forms of suicide carried out as acts of *protest* against civil authorities. Professor Jan Yün-hua, who has carefully documented these, comments:

> Such men were monks who used the violent act of self-destruction as a protest against the political oppression and persecution of their religion.[29]

Although the number of such instances was never great, the Chinese historical records are clear on this matter. Those Mahayanists who defended such practices pointed to the documented ease and tranquility with which such self-immolators died and to the sacrifice itself which brought light—moral and spiritual light—into contexts of great darkness.

And it was, of course, this Chinese tradition that was known to the monks of Vietnam who in 1963 felt the time had come for them to register their own ultimate form of protest. The continuity in the details is striking; just as in the text of the Lotus Sutra and in the examples from Chinese history, so too the monks of Vietnam did not simply burn themselves to death but did so while seated in the lotus posture and while engaged in meditation. To that extent their death, even while engulfed in flames and surrounded by the violence of a society at war, was in the pattern of the exemplary great death of Śākyamuni. It was executed with full clarity of mind and the exercise of the will; in that sense, it was very traditional.

But it also happened in a very public place, one where there were loudspeakers and even foreign journalists present. As such it could not possibly be isolated as a purely private act on the part of the monk—especially one acting to "negate" the world. As public as it was, it was a highly visible act played out on the stage of the world; it clearly said something about that monk's concern not only for his sangha but also for his fellow countrymen. And, of course, it had consequences. It was a factor in the attitude of many concerning the war being fought; it had an effect on the minds, and then later the actions, of people thousands of miles away. Having learned much from Paul Mus, probably our century's most astute scholar-observer of Buddhism in Southeast Asia, Frances FitzGerald wrote:

> By taking the pose of the Buddha, Quang Duc was indicating to both Viet-

---

[29] Jan Yün-hua, "Buddhist Self-immolation in Medieval China," *History of Religions,* Vol. 4, no. 2 (Winter 1965), 252.

Buddhist Engulfed by Flames *From 8th century Japanese painting.*

namese and Americans a morality and a responsibility for others that lay beyond the divisions of political systems and culture.[30]

Given the variety of their traditions, it has been and will probably remain impossible to see any tight and necessary linkup between Buddhism and any specific sociopolitical system. The record of the past is as mixed as that of any world religion. Sometimes Buddhists have expressed great distress under a given political system and have begun movements that gave expression to their longing for a more just and equitable society on this earth.[31] Sometimes, especially in Theravada countries, the ancient model of the benevolent King Asoka inspired more recent rulers

---

[30] Frances FitzGerald, *Fire in the Lake: The Vietnamese and the Americans in Vietnam* (New York: Vintage Books, 1972), p. 179.

[31] See Daniel L. Overmyer, *Folk Buddhist Religion: Dissenting Sects in Late Traditional China* (Cambridge, Mass.: Harvard University Press, 1976), and Hue-Tam Ho Tai, *Millenarianism and Peasant Politics in Vietnam* (Cambridge, Mass.: Harvard University Press, 1983).

to follow his example.[32] This was also an important element in the development of a Buddhist socialism in Burma in the 1960s under the aegis of U Nu.[33] Some Buddhists have claimed to find affinities between Buddhism and Marxism; others have been just as vocal in denying that such could exist. Some Buddhists find communist states objectionable because they severely restrict the free exercise of religion. Others find capitalism objectionable because it seems systematically to intensify and exaggerate the greed and craving (thirst, *tṛṣṇā*) that are already so much a part of our human problem, both as individuals and as societies.

As far as the degree to which the sangha is willing to involve itself directly in social and political problems, it would be a mistake to make too simple a distinction between the Theravada and Mahayana traditions. Certainly if things in a given society are relatively just and peaceful, the sangha will much prefer to carry on in its traditional ways: not only seeking nirvana as a far-off goal but also exemplifying and articulating it in present society as much as possible. When even more expression than that seems needed, members of the sangha may react as they see fit.

Perhaps in the twentieth century as never before in history the Buddhist sangha has had to readjust to changing images of itself as a lotus in a pool of mud. In traditional Buddhist contexts this was a powerful symbol of the Buddha: a pure-white, unsullied flower that blooms in a swamp so muddy its bottom cannot be seen. Some Buddhists have preferred to call attention to the *whiteness* of the blossom; they said that it is not only a model of the Buddha but also a normative one for the sangha itself. They have concluded that the sangha should remain true to its tradition of detached meditation, unsullied with the mud of worldly affairs. Others have said that the importance of the lotus lies in the fact that it is open to the world and at its base is *connected* with the mud of the world; they conclude that the sangha has an obligation to ameliorate all ways men suffer, even social causes for that pain. They conclude that this cannot be done unless the world itself is entered and engaged.

---

[32] See essays in *Religion and Legitimation of Power in Thailand, Laos, and Burma,* ed. by Bardwell L. Smith (Chambersburg, Pa.: Anima Books, 1978).

[33] E. Sarkisyanz, *Buddhist Backgrounds of the Burmese Revolution* (The Hague: Martinus Nijhoff, 1965).

8

conclusion

During the 1690s a Dutch physician named Englebert Kaempfer was in Japan as part of a group of his countrymen there. Having earlier visited part of what used to be called Siam but is now Thailand, Kaempfer wrote a treatise, *The History of Japan Together with a Description of the Kingdom of Siam,* which was read by others in Europe. In describing the religion he found practiced by the Japanese, he wrote the following, a hypothesis that must have struck many of his fellow Europeans as bold and scarcely believable:

> The origine of this religion, which quickly spread thro' most Asiatick countries to the very extremities of the East, (not unlike the Indian fig-tree which propagates itself, and spreads far round by sending down new roots from the extremities of its branches,) must be look'd for among the Brahmines [of India]. I have strong reasons to believe, both from the affinity of the name, and the very nature of this religion, that its author and founder is the very same person, whom the Brahmines call Budha, and believe to be an essential part of Wisthnu [= Visnu], or their Deity, who made its ninth appearance in the world under this name, and in the shape of this man. The Chinese and Japanese call him Buds and Siaka [= Śākyamuni].[1]

In this Kaempfer expressed his hunch that through Buddhism there was an histori-

---

[1] Englebert Kaempfer, *The History of Japan Together with a Description of the Kingdom of Siam, 1690-1692,* Vol. 2, trans. by J. G. Schéuchzer (Glasgow: James MacLehose and Sons, 1906), p. 56.

cal connection between India and Japan. He was not the first to guess that such a connection existed, but it was his publication of this hypothesis in Europe that received significant attention.

From the tone and tentative nature of Kaempfer's remark, it is clear that he himself was not entirely sure that the religion he had seen both in Thailand and in Japan were essentially the same and had a common parentage in India. He was unsure, as no doubt many others were at that time. After all, Japan on the eastern end of Asia seemed so totally different, not only in language but also in culture from Thailand. To suppose that, in spite of the immense geographical and cultural difference between them, they still shared a common religious philosophy was in some ways to fly in the face of what seemed to be common sense.

During the 300 years between Kaempfer and ourselves, his guess has been proven correct over and over again. A prodigious amount of scholarship on the history of Buddhism has been carried out. Many of the most important sutras and other texts have been studied and translated into the languages of Europe. Scholars have compared the scriptures that exist in the various canonical languages. Like the other "world" religions, Buddhism traveled far in part because it was a literate tradition and at least in some ways could be transmitted by the written word. But traditions are always more than books; earlier travelers in Buddhist cultures came back with reports, sometimes very valuable and sometimes strangely filtered through preexisting stereotypes. In more recent years the fuller study of Buddhism has also had to use persons trained in anthropology who have gone into Buddhist cultures, interviewing people who profess to have taken refuge in the Three Treasures and studying the impact of Buddhism on their daily lives.

Then too there are those Westerners who have not only studied Buddhism but also in one way or another have been sufficiently impressed by the Middle Path to think of themselves as Buddhists. Their insights from that experience and level of participation have added another new dimension to the West's ever-growing knowledge of this ancient religious tradition. Nevertheless, our knowledge remains partial. Many important texts have not yet been adequately studied or translated. Portions of the historical account still remain blank or are dimly perceived. The politics of the twentieth century have made the continuity of the sangha in certain places problematic and access to it on the part of Westerners equally so.

Within some Buddhist texts themselves there are predictions about phases through which the dharma goes; some Buddhists—but not all—hold that this suggests that for whole periods of time it goes into partial and then total eclipse in some places. They say that that is what happened in India and may be happening elsewhere in Asia today. Others, usually European and American Buddhists eager to detect the signs of transmission to their own cultures, often claim that the dharma's decline in one place signals its growing strength somewhere else. Unless one is much more of a clairvoyant than I, however, these things of the future must remain unknowable.

bibliography

SOURCES AND TEXTS

LING, T. O., *A Dictionary of Buddhism,* New York: Charles Scribner's Sons, 1972.

REYNOLDS, FRANK E., *Guide to the Buddhist Religion,* Boston, Mass.: G. K. Hall and Co., 1981.

CONZE, E., *Buddhist Texts Through the Ages,* New York: Harper & Row, 1954.

DEBARY, W. T., ed., *Buddhist Tradition in India, China, and Japan,* New York: Random House (Vintage), 1972.

WARREN, HENRY CLARK, ed., *Buddhism in Translations,* Cambridge, Mass.: Harvard University Press, 1896 and New York: Atheneum, 1969.

EARLY AND INDIAN BUDDHISM

NAKAMURA, HAJIME, *Gotama Buddha,* Chatsworth, Calif.: Buddhist Books International, 1977.

RAHULA, WALPOLA, *What the Buddha Taught,* New York: Grove Press, 1974.

CONZE, E., *Buddhist Thought in India,* Ann Arbor, Mich.: University of Michigan Press, 1967.

DUTT, SUKUMAR, *Buddhist Monks and Monasteries of India,* London: George Allen and Unwin, 1962.

DAYAL, HAL, *The Bodhisattva Doctrine in Buddhist Sanskrit Literature,* London: Kegan Paul, 1932.

SRI LANKA AND SOUTHEAST ASIA

SMITH, BARDWELL L., *The Two Wheels of the Dhamma*, Chambersburg, Pa.: American Academy of Religion, 1972.

CARRITHERS, MICHAEL, *The Forest Monks of Sri Lanka: An Anthropological and Historical Study,* Delhi: Oxford University Press, 1983.

NYANAPONIKA, THERA, *The Heart of Buddhist Meditation,* New York: Samuel Weiser, Inc., 1962.

SPIRO, MELFORD E., *Buddhism and Society: A Great Tradition and Its Burmese Vicissitudes,* New York: Harper & Row, 1971.

CHINA

CH'EN, KENNETH, *Buddhism in China: A Historical Survey,* Princeton, N.J.: Princeton University Press, 1964.

MIURA, ISSHŪ and RUTHER FULLER SASAKI, *Zen Dust: The History of the Koan and Koan Study in Rinzai (Lin-Chi) Zen,* New York: Harcourt, Brace, and World, 1966.

WRIGHT, ARTHUR F., *Buddhism in Chinese History,* New York: Atheneum, 1968.

WELCH, HOLMES, *The Practice of Chinese Buddhism 1900–1950,* Cambridge, Mass.: Harvard University Press, 1967.

TIBET

DALAI LAMA XIVTH, *My Land and My People,* New York: McGraw-Hill, 1962.

HOPKINS, JEFFREY, *Tantra in Tibet,* London: George Allen and Unwin, 1978.

THURMAN, ROBERT, trans., *The Holy Teaching of Vimalakirti,* University Park, Pa.: Pennsylvania State University Press, 1976.

STEIN, R. A., *Tibetan Civilization,* Stanford, Calif.: Stanford University Press, 1972.

KOREA

BUSWELL, ROBERT E., trans., *The Korean Approach to Zen: The Collected Works of Chinul,* Honolulu: University of Hawaii Press, 1983.

LEE, PETER H., trans., *Lives of Eminent Korean Monks,* Cambridge, Mass.: Harvard University Press, 1969.

PARK, SUNG BAE, *Buddhist Faith and Sudden Enlightenment,* Albany, N.Y.: State University of New York Press, 1983.

JAPAN

COLLCUTT, MARTIN, *Five Mountains: The Rinzai Zen Monastic Institution in Medieval Japan,* Cambridge, Mass.: Harvard University Press, 1981.

KITAGAWA, JOSEPH M., *Religion in Japanese History,* New York: Columbia University Press, 1966.

LA FLEUR, WILLIAM R., *The Karma of Words: Buddhism and the Literary Arts in Medieval Japan,* Berkeley and Los Angeles, Calif.: University of California Press, 1983.

SUZUKI, DAISETZ T., *The Training of a Zen Buddhist Monk,* New York: New York University Books, 1959 (Kyoto: The Eastern Buddhist Society, 1934).

HISAMATSU, SHIN'ICHI, *Zen and the Fine Arts,* New York and Tokyo: Kodansha International, 1974.

BUDDHISM AND THE WEST

ABE, MASAO, *Zen and Western Thought,* Honolulu: University of Hawaii Press, 1985.

SMART, NINIAN, *A Dialogue of Religions,* London: SCM Press, 1960.

PREBISH, CHARLES S., *American Buddhism,* Belmont, Calif.: Duxbury, 1979.

DUMOULIN, H., ed., *Buddhism in the Modern World,* New York: Macmillan, 1976.

YUASA, YASUO, *The Body: Toward an Eastern Mind-Body Theory*, Albany, N.Y.: State University of New York Press, 1987.

Index